T0171068

#SUCCESS

Mastering the Basics to a Happy,
Healthy, and Wealthy Life

CARLA SCHESSER

BALBOA.
PRESS

A DIVISION OF HAY HOUSE

Balboa Press books may be ordered through booksellers or by contacting:

Balboa Press
A Division of Hay House
1663 Liberty Drive
Bloomington, IN 47403
www.balboapress.com.au
1 (877) 407-4847

Printed in the United States of America.

ISBN: 978-1-4525-1184-9 (sc)
ISBN: 978-1-4525-1185-6 (e)

Balboa Press rev. date: 10/08/2013

TABLE OF CONTENTS

INTRODUCTION

Do you ever find yourself questioning your life path?

Do you ever wonder if this is all there is to life?

Do you sometimes wonder if there isn't something far greater to be experienced with your time here on Earth?

Do you sometimes feel that you're tiptoeing through life not allowing yourself to be all that you know you can be?

You aren't alone. There are many of us young adults today that are struggling to figure out what we want to do in life and how we want to do it. We are constantly bombarded with the word *"should"* and it is taking its toll on our decisions:

- You should go to University
- You should get a good degree so you can live a good life

- <u>You should find a safe and secure job</u>
- <u>You should find a mate and have some children</u>
- <u>You should, you should, you should</u>

These are the statements influencing us in subtle ways to follow the normal, socially accepted path, but when we take a deep look inside ourselves we often find that this isn't what we desire. We want something much greater.

I have certainly had my fair share of difficulties throughout my short time here on this planet. I was born with a rare disease; my muscles would not grow, my spine was fused stiff, and it was and still is incredibly hard to gain and maintain weight. My mother was told that I would never walk and that I would live a very troubled life because of this disease.

The first few months of my life were spent almost entirely inside my physiotherapist's office as my mother would not accept what she considered to be the *'opinion'* of the doctors. She stubbornly insisted that I would live a normal life and it is because of this refusal to accept 'opinions' that I eventually took my first steps at 19 months and have been walking ever since.

That isn't the end of the story though, the pain endured. Even though I could walk I was always the smallest kid by far in school and my peers were mean and relentless. I was constantly teased and bullied for being the 'midget kid' and this harassment continued throughout my entire academic career. High school was the worst and it was at this time, after the years and years of verbal abuse and constant conditioning that I was abnormal, that I seriously considered ending my own life. Obviously I chose not to take my life and I'm extremely grateful to my past self for making that decision. It was through this unbearable pain that I was introduced to my true calling in life and this book was born.

I don't tell you this story to gain your pity; in fact, that is the absolute last thing I want. I tell you my story to let you know that I too have been through some extremely difficult times in my life. Every person on this Earth has a story, whether it's a bad childhood, poor decision making, physical or mental disability, loss of loved ones, etc. No matter who we are one thing is for certain, and that is that there will always be suffering at some point in life. However, the difference between those that succeed in life and those that fail is what is made of the suffering. Pain is unavoidable and it shouldn't be feared, but it is necessary that you use your pain in constructive ways or your quality of life will suffer forever.

I've written this book for you and inside you'll find:

- Lessons and knowledge that I've gathered over the past eight years of extensive self-study

- Advice my many successful mentors have passed down to me
- How to find and live your life purpose
- Mental attitudes that practically guarantee a successful life
- Strategies for building and growing your riches
- How to experience the true joy of living every single day
- And so much more

There really is no better book to introduce you to the field of personal development; after all, in order to live more you need to become more as a person. It is through my own personal development pursuits that I transformed my pain into joy and it is with these experiences that I desire to help you do the same.

Life is too short to live on someone else's terms; this is our life and if we don't decide what to do with it then we'll end up like everybody else, mediocre with no ambition. It's time for us to stop playing follow the follower and rise up and claim our power to create a life that fills us with inspiration and enthusiasm.

It's time that we live our lives as we want and inside you'll find the exact strategies that I've used to do so for myself. Let's dig in!

*Note—Accompanying most of the chapters in this book will be worksheets that I've created to help you better understand the topics. You can find those resources and many more on my website: http://carlaschesser.com.au/resources/

SECTION 1
THE BEGINNING

1.1

CHAPTER 1:
THE PATH WITH A HEART

1.1.1. The Quiet Voice of Discontent

You've followed all of the rules and you've done everything that everyone has told you to do. You've listened to those whose opinions you value. Maybe you did well in high school, maybe you didn't but you made it to University and decided upon a major. You're nearing the end of your schooling and you feel that you should be excited, but for some reason you're not. You feel that you should be satisfied with where you are, but you're not. You feel that you should be happy with your life and where it's headed, but you're not.

Inside there is this nagging, clawing feeling that something is missing. No matter how hard you try to quiet this feeling through partying, hanging with friends, t.v., drugs and alcohol, it persists. It's uncomfortable. It feels like an overwhelming anxiety could bubble up to the surface at any time and completely consume you in its wrath.

You are not alone. I went through this same thing myself and there are countless others going through it as well. This inescapable feeling is the voice of your inner being. It is the real you, the you which you have never known before. Some call it a soul, some call it God, but it does not matter what you call it, what's important is that it's beckoning you towards becoming the magnificent, powerful being you were meant to be.

Millions of people go through their entire lives moving from distraction to distraction in order to avoid facing their inner being and deepest fears. They drown it out as best they can by filling their life with meaningless, mundane activities and their well-being suffers for it. It's apparent that the majority of people are not living as the human beings they are capable of being, they live lives of "quiet desperation" as Thoreau said, aimlessly following the pack and doing what they're told.

This isn't you. You know that you want more out of life but you're afraid to admit it. You're afraid to admit that the accepted life path isn't for you. I want you to know that it's okay to admit this and that this is the first step towards the most magnificent life experience you could ever have on this planet.

It's time for you to look your fears in the eye and conquer them, one by one. It's okay to be afraid and admit it, but it's not okay to be afraid and hide from your fears. We're all afraid of some things and what makes someone a success in my book is someone who is willing to face those fears head on and work through them little by little. If we simply sit back and maintain the status quo, if we ignore that small voice within us, we allow our fears to keep us trapped inside the small cage that we have always known.

It's as if for our whole lives we've been living inside a small closet without ever knowing the outside world. Of course we're going to be scared whenever we even begin to think about opening up that closet door and stepping outside, but as you and I both know, there isn't anything that scary about the outside world. Our fears are illogical and if we so much as submit to them once, we reinforce their power and continue to remain enslaved by them. We must follow the small voice within us that knows our true path in life regardless of what emotions we may feel; our happiness depends upon it.

So what are you afraid of? What are the chains that bind you that you're rarely aware of? I'll tell you mine:

- I'm afraid of being so different that nobody will like me
- I'm afraid of succeeding and people becoming jealous of me
- I'm afraid of giving it my all and falling flat on my face
- I'm afraid of being rejected by those around me
- I'm afraid of being alone

Whenever you look underneath all of these you can see that they all come down to one basic fear, and that is the fear of not being connected with the people and world around me. We are social beings at our core and the fear of being alone is one of the greatest fears that we will ever have to face. I want you to know that these fears and any other fears you may have are completely valid, but I also want you to know that they may be exactly what is holding you back from living a life you love.

1.1.2. Conformity

You have most likely spent the majority of your life following the crowd and trying your best to fit in. We were all raised to behave like sheep since the day we were born; trained to blindly follow the sheep in front of and around us without questioning where we're going.

There are people that have broken away from the herd and have taken control of their destinies but when we see them they often frighten us. They make us feel uneasy because they remind us of who we could be if summoned the courage to break away from the pack. These rare individuals are the people that have embraced their own uniqueness and are absolutely okay with being who they are regardless of what anyone else may think about them. They are the movers and shakers in the history of humanity; they are the Einstein's, the Edison's, and the Gates'; they are the people that stop and question the commonly accepted and then take off in their own direction of what they feel is best.

I'm going to ask you a few questions and I want you to take the time to really think about them:

- What kind of results do you see the majority of people getting in their lives?
- Are most people truly happy and fulfilled?
- Do they have great relationships?
- Are they enjoying financial abundance?
- Are they doing work they love?
- Are they in incredible shape physically?

If you're honest with yourself, you'll admit that the average person is not enjoying very good results in any area of his or her life. This is because average to poor results are considered the 'norm' for our society and the herd will always embrace the idea of 'normalcy'.

The social norm is to:

1. Go to University and get good grades
2. Get a "secure" job with great benefits
3. Have a family
4. Work forty hours a week until you are sixty five or older
5. Slowly atrophy until the day of your death

That may sound depressing but that's the truth isn't it? Isn't that the exact life plan that's been laid out for you? Doesn't a life that follows that path sound miserable? It certainly does to me.

Why do we follow this life plan and accept it as best way to go? Is there another way to live that doesn't suck? Yes, there really is, but it requires courage and a willingness to break away from the pack and be your own person.

There is a way to live that results in:

• extreme fulfilment with life
• outstanding health

- deep and connected relationships
- financial abundance
- unbelievable levels of happiness

You want to experience these in your life, but before you can you must first realize that following the herd will never get you there.

I want you to realize the stupidity of doing things just because that's what everyone else is doing. You have a brain in your head and you are more than capable of making your own life choices. You have the ability to think for yourself and decide what would be best for you and your life.

Often you don't trust yourself and you allow other's ideas to take priority over your own. Instead of listening to your heart, you listen to your parent's advice and go to University and get a <u>safe</u> job. You settle down, marry, have a few kids, and then slowly wait out your days until the grim reaper comes to take you from this Earth forever.

How do you want to live your life until the day you die? Do you want to barely scrape by and do things that you hate doing? Or would you rather wake up with absolute enthusiasm everyday and go to bed with the biggest smile on your face?

Do you want to work at a meaningless job crunching numbers all day? Or would you rather do something that makes a difference in the world?

From the deepest depths of my heart I want you to know that it's okay to be different and pursue a path that totally excites you. It doesn't matter what that path is and it doesn't matter if it's not 'traditional'; what does matter is doing what you absolutely love every single day. If you pursue your heart's desires with everything you've got everything else in your life will fall into place. This doesn't mean that it will be easy or fast; in fact, it will be much more difficult than going the 'normal' route, but it's so much more satisfying and I can one hundred percent guarantee that.

1.1.3. The Way Out

There is a way out of the herd but you should know up front that it isn't easy and it will require more courage than you've ever exercised before.

The only way out is through a commitment to that small voice within. It's the voice that tells you about all of the magnificent things you can accomplish; it's the voice that speaks up every time you conform; it's the voice that always knows exactly what to do in any given moment; it's the voice that you often want to ignore because listening would result in drastic changes to your lifestyle.

The first step in committing to your inner voice is figuring out what 'success' means to you. You've been taught your entire life that success means lots of money, a huge house, a sweet sports car, a luxurious yacht, and all the fame that you could ever desire. We lust after these ideas without a second thought as if they are the end all be all to life; however, these ideas are not what success is unless this is how you choose to define success. If you do not consciously define what success means to you, you will accept the status quo by default. Bearing that in mind, glance over the questions below; can you see clearly, without a doubt, the things you will strive to achieve?

- So what does the word 'success' mean to you?
- Imagine that you are on your death bed looking back on your life . . . how will you know that your life was a good one?
- Does it mean that you helped as many people as possible?
- Does it mean that you earned as much money and collected as many things as possible?
- Does it mean that you did your best and grasped every opportunity that presented itself?

Take some time right now to think seriously about these questions and your answers. There are no right or wrong answers, but make sure that you feel strongly about what you do decide upon. Your answers to these questions will act as a compass from this day forward with which you can make better life decisions.

Earl Nightingale defined success as **"the progressive realization of a worthy idea".** This is a powerful definition because it shows us that success isn't just a destination, but a journey. This means that as soon as you define what you want in life and begin working towards it you are successful.

The next step in following the small voice within is identifying your life purpose. This is an idea very closely related to success but this focuses on what you feel your purpose is for being here on this planet at this particular time.

- Why are you here right now?
- What do you have to offer to the rest of the world?
- What possible reason could there be for your existence?

Living a life purpose that you decide upon will bring immense fulfilment into your life. For the first time, you will know exactly what to do with your life without having to depend on the opinions of those around you.

There are two fundamental states of being for everything in the Universe; the first is growth, and the second is decay. If you are not growing then by default you are decaying. This reveals to us the importance of ensuring that we are growing throughout our entire lives, for as soon as we stop we immediately begin to die.

Stagnation and complacency are the indicators that you are allowing yourself to decay. As a young adult you are likely learning at a rapid pace and this keeps you in a state of growth. However, it's very common that once individuals get out of university they decide that they are done learning because they have finished school. This is a major mistake and the cause of the state of decay that you see all around you. You see those around you, perhaps your family or older friends, repeat the same routines day after day and you know that you don't want that. You know that you want to continue to develop throughout your entire lifetime because growth is the ultimate joy of life.

Ultimately, if you want to be completely happy in this life experience you must completely embrace the idea of growth. It does not matter where you currently are and it does not matter where you will eventually be; there will always be another plateau to reach or another mountain to climb. It is the climbing of these personal mountains that is the joy of life which will lead you to the much greener pastures.

1.2

CHAPTER 2:
AN INTRODUCTION TO
PERSONAL DEVELOPMENT

1.2.1. The Philosophy

So what is personal development? At its essence, **personal development is a consistent, sincere effort to better one's self in all areas of life**.

The definition is extremely broad because there are so many different options to pursue within personal development as a whole. You could work on developing yourself mentally, spiritually, emotionally, or physically, and the gains you experience in any one of these areas will translate into every other.

My favourite thing about personal development is that there isn't just one correct path, there are options and with options comes freedom.

I used to fall into the trap of thinking that I had to develop in only certain areas that were 'good' or 'noble'. I had the idea in my mind that I should only develop spiritually, because all other areas were physical and therefore somehow less important than spiritual development. So I forced myself to focus on areas where I didn't feel drawn to grow and my growth was therefore much slower than it could have been. Over time however, I found that we should always focus our attention on what attracts us the most, as it is these areas that contain the valuable lessons we need at particular times in our life.

If the idea of advancing yourself financially is what excites you then so be it! That's awesome, go for it and give it all you've got! Just because some people would label money as *evil* or *bad* doesn't negate it as a valid pursuit of personal development. You'll find that as you follow your attraction you'll learn a tremendous amount about yourself and the world around you that will make you an overall better person.

The philosophy of personal development really comes down to the idea that we exist here on this planet for the purpose of growth, development, and evolution.

As we discussed earlier, everything in the Universe is either growing or decaying and if you aren't growing then by necessity you are decaying. If we are alive and well then it makes sense that our primary focus should be that of developing ourselves.

It's obvious that when we die we lose everything of a physical nature; no matter how bad we want to we cannot bring our money, possessions, or relationships with us into whatever lies beyond this life. The only possible thing that can persist after physical death is consciousness. Personal development is concerned with the development of consciousness and is therefore the most intelligent focus for our lives.

1.2.2. Why Should I Care?

So why should you care about personal development? Personal development enhances the world around you and the people around you but it's also a very selfish pursuit (in a good way). There is no better feeling than making a break through in your life that elevates you to new levels of existence.

Ultimately, your satisfaction with life is based upon your growth. If you allow yourself to remain stagnant, life loses its exciting flavour and existence becomes dull and mundane; it is growth that keeps things fresh and new.

You will have to find your own reasons for pursuing personal development as the motivation is different with each person. All I can do is share with you my own experiences, brought about through trial and error.

In my life, I've experienced two distinct periods that can be defined as complacency and growth. I've cycled back and forth between the two for years but I now know that I've reached a tipping point where I can never slide back into complacency. Whenever I am at a stand-still and I'm not pushing myself to get better, I get depressed very quickly. Perhaps this is a good thing and perhaps it's not, but it is what it is. If I don't push forward I get extremely bored and the longer I stay standing still the less joy I experience.

On the flip side, when I am pushing forward and making serious improvements I feel absolutely magnificent. I feel powerful, alive, and joyful; I feel like I'm doing something worthwhile and I'm having fun doing it. It feels as if I'm playing a thrilling game, the game of life, and there's nothing I'd rather do than level up my character and tackle bigger and bigger challenges.

I love seeing the progression from one state of being to another. I love looking back on my life, just a short six months ago and seeing how far I've come. I love the feeling of doing my best to solve problems and tackle challenges to move to new plateaus in life. I love starting out as a beginner and advancing to mastery in particular domains in life.

I enjoy the hard work that personal development requires; it's fun to test myself and see where my real limits are. It's fun to break away from the pack and apply my entire being to this life experience to see just what I can do. I love moving from feeling lazy and incompetent to powerful and confident. I love recognizing my true power and the power of everyone else around me. I love looking my fears in the eye and running towards them as I break them down one by one so I can live as who I was meant to be. I absolutely love personal development.

These are the feelings that I want to share with you; I want you to feel the same way about your life. I want you to wake up every morning and practically jump out of bed because you're so excited to get moving towards your goals and dreams. I want you to know your own limitless potential and exactly what you're capable of. I want you to know your worth as a human being and realize that no matter what has happened in your life you are worthy of the best this Universe has to offer. I want you to feel good about yourself. I want you to feel that your life matters and that you have the ability to make this world a better place.

Imagine how great this Earth would be if we all felt this way. Imagine what it would be like if every single person woke up and was enthusiastic about their day because they were doing what they absolutely loved to do. Imagine how happy this place could be!

This may seem like a far-fetched dream to you but I know that it is possible and I know that we can get there. I know that we don't have to do things we don't want to do just because that's the way it's always been done.

It is your time! It is your generation that is beginning to realize the insanity of the way they are told to live their lives! They know that there is more to life than settling down and living a quiet, desperate existence until the day of their death! But what about you?

All it takes is for each of us to rise up and live the life that we know we want to live. That means something different for every person and that's the beauty of human uniqueness. I know that through my own personal development efforts I satisfy myself and help make the world a better place; what more could you ask for than making yourself feel good and helping those around you at the same time? It's a win-win situation for everyone and that's exactly what personal development is all about.

1.2.3. Personal Development is not Easy!

You'll find one extremely important message throughout this entire book and that message is:

There is no such thing as <u>something</u> for <u>nothing</u>!

Unfortunately, the most common mindset in our society today is one that expects to receive something great for little or no effort. This mindset goes against the basic laws of the Universe, such as the law that says for every action there will be an opposite and equal reaction. What you get out of life will always be proportionate to the amount of effort that you put in. So many of us are looking for non-existent shortcuts and this searching is what causes much of our frustration.

You can see this every time you turn on a t.v. and watch the commercials that come on. Inevitably, you'll see commercials that are trying to sell you incredible health, fabulous wealth, and the love of your life all in a magic pill that only costs $19.99. This simply isn't so! **No worthwhile results can ever be enjoyed without first putting forth labour.** There is no shortcut and no easy path to what you want in life.

The results of serious personal growth efforts are some of the best to be enjoyed in the entire Universe. You can have sky high self-esteem, loving relationships, abundance finances, and much more if you'll only put forth the effort required.

All of this goes to say that **personal development is NOT easy!** In fact, it's likely the hardest thing you will ever do in your life.

I don't say these things to scare you away from personal development, rather to give you a very realistic idea of what to expect. If you begin your journey of personal growth with expectations of ease then you'll very likely quit as soon as the going gets a little tough (which it most certainly will). By understanding what lays ahead of you, you are much more likely to persist until the rewards are yours to enjoy.

Personal growth isn't a magic-pill solution to the problems in your life, even though it's often marketed as such. It won't be quick and it won't be painless. You will struggle, you will sweat and you will feel like giving up, but if you simply persist you will enjoy what so few of those on Earth ever do. The greatest rewards will always be reserved for those that put in the sincere effort.

I know that as you read these words you may be turned off from the idea of personal development and that's okay. Use your imagination and ponder what life might be like if you really took the time to develop yourself to a high degree. Build an image of what you want your life to be like, realize you can achieve it, and then set out on developing yourself until you are strong enough to make it a reality.

It's awesome that personal development is so hard because it is only through difficulty that we can truly understand our strength. If everything was easy we would never grow stronger as human beings and life would be insanely boring. It is the challenge and growth experienced that makes life worth living, and there's nothing like personal development which will stimulate this experience more.

Prepare yourself for the journey ahead and muster the courage to take the first step, for the first step is always the hardest. Once you get going and build some momentum, keep it going. Focus on what's directly in front of you and keep your feet moving; crawl if you have to but always move forward. Before you know it you'll look back on where you are today and be absolutely amazed at how far you've come.

Before we move ahead I want to emphasize that you cannot and should not attempt to implement everything in this book at one time. Due to the difficulty of personal development work you can only tackle so many areas in your life at once. If you attempt too much at one time you will end up overwhelmed, frustrated, and you'll eventually give up on your pursuits. Keep this in mind as you move through this book and begin thinking about which area of your life you would like to master first.

SECTION 2
THE MIDDLE

2.1

CHAPTER 3:
YOUR MARVELOUS MIND

2.1.1. Introduction

Your mind is one of the most mysterious and extraordinary things in the known Universe. You have been blessed with a powerful tool adequate to fulfil your every desire if you'll only learn exactly how to use it.

Why do we place so little importance on the mind? Why do so few of us take the time to learn about our minds and how they operate? An obvious answer is that our minds have been given to us for free and we often place little value on what's been handed to us. The mind is also an invisible entity and it's somewhat difficult to study that which we cannot sense. The fact is, the mind is very under-studied and underutilized and the result is the current state of our society.

The most successful individuals, those that are living happy, abundant, healthy lives, are those that have learned how to put their minds to good use. They took the time and put forth the effort required to learn how to use their mind and the fruits of their labour are apparent.

You cannot achieve anything worthwhile in this life without utilising your mind to its fullest capabilities. You must constantly push yourself past the limitations restraining you so that you may grow stronger and more capable with each passing year. As soon as we stop learning and growing, we start dying.

This chapter and the proceeding one will provide you an aerial view of your mind, its parts, and how it operates so that you may begin putting its magnificent powers to work in your life.

2.1.2. Success is Ninety Percent Mental

Ninety percent of success in any walk of life is a direct result of how the mind is used. Top athletes, top business executives, top parents, top entrepreneurs, and the most successful individuals all understand the important truth that the mind is what counts.

It really is as simple as Henry Ford said, "If you think you can do a thing or think you can't do a thing, you're right"". We often fail before we ever begin an undertaking because we use our minds in the wrong way. We use past failures, imaginary fears, and feelings of unworthiness to scare us away from pursuing our biggest dreams. There is no prerequisite for success in life except for the hundred percent belief in yourself and your abilities.

Learning how to cultivate complete belief or faith is one of the challenges that stands in the way between where you are and where you most wish to be. It takes consistent effort to *convince* yourself that you are capable of succeeding. You can't tell yourself that you believe in your abilities just one or two times and expect it to make a real difference; you have got to affirm your belief in yourself day after day, month after month, until it becomes an unbreakable habit.

When you reach the point of having complete faith in yourself you will know it. There is a noticeable rush of positive energy throughout the entire body that lets you know that in this moment, you do in fact believe in yourself. Use this knowledge of the positive emotion to gauge whether or not you believe in yourself at any moment in time.

The human mind literally creates our world. Take a look around you and think about everything you see . . . Everything that has ever been created, from the chair you're sitting in to the lights above you, were first created in the mind of one individual. Contemplate this fact, the implications are huge! This means that literally *anything* your mind can conceive and most importantly, believe, it can create.

You might think that this is some bogus *'positive thinking'* strategy that you've probably heard so much about. I urge you to hold off on making snap judgments until you experiment with the power of positive thinking in your own life; you will be pleasantly surprised by the results.

Up to this point we have never had a way to scientifically explain the power of thought, but the field of quantum physics is now doing just that. The great mystics and philosophers throughout time, including Jesus, Buddha, William James, and Marcus Aurelius, have always known and taught the power of the mind, but as westernized scientific societies we couldn't go on blind faith alone. Quantum physics is the result of our curiosity about the Universe and our desire to understand how it works on a scientific level.

What quantum physics is uncovering is that one's perceptions and beliefs about reality actually alter reality to fit that perspective. This is huge!

For example, scientists have performed experiments attempting to discover whether the basic building blocks of our Universe are either particles or waves. They argued and argued as each scientist obtained different results whenever the experiment was performed, and eventually they took a step back and began experimenting in a new way. They discovered that the fundamental building blocks became waves or particles depending on the expectations of the scientist doing the experimenting. If the scientist expected them to be particles, that's what they appeared as; if the scientist expected them to be waves, that's what they appeared as.

This new understanding of our world has yet to make it to the mainstream individual. Thus, people continue to believe that their reality is the way it is because of something beyond their control when, in fact, their reality is the way it is because of the specific way they expect it to be.

Kind of funny huh?

This explains why the most successful individuals place so much importance on their minds. They realize that they create their own reality by their beliefs and so they throw their full efforts into cultivating a mindset

CARLA SCHESSER

that inevitably leads them to the phenomenal success they enjoy. While the average person forever blames people and circumstances for their failures, the successful individual always looks within for the source of both achievement and failure.

I have but one question for you: If your success in life is almost entirely a result of how you use your mind, how much time are you devoting to developing it?

Answer: Probably not enough.

2.1.3. The Two Parts of the Mind

Now that you understand how important your mind is to your success in life, it's time to learn what the mind is and how it operates.

There are two sections to your mind; the conscious, and the subconscious. Let's cover each in detail.

The Conscious Mind

The conscious section of your mind is who you think of yourself as. This is the area where you do your thinking and your planning; it is the place of logic. You are quite familiar with this part of your mind as it is most likely this that you are learning to use as your life moves forward.

The crazy thing is, your conscious mind performs only 1-5% of the work of the mind! This may seem like an exaggeration but it is not; your conscious mind is like the driver at the wheel of a great big crane, it directs and controls the crane, but it does not do any of the actual work. The same thing is true of your conscious mind, it is the driver at the wheel of your incredibly powerful subconscious mind.

Willpower originates in the conscious mind and this is why it is so limited in what it can accomplish. Have you ever tried to accomplish a goal or change a habit with pure willpower (for example, have you tried to lose weight, stop smoking, take up daily exercise or anything along those lines?). If you have then you know that using only willpower is a poor strategy for creating change in your life. When you attempt use your willpower to make a change you are only using 1-5% of your resources and that makes it physically taxing and near impossible!

Learning to effectively utilize your conscious mind to direct your subconscious mind is what living a successful life is all about. The top performers that we talked about in the last section have learned how to do this, whether they can tell you how they do it or not is another question altogether. This is the challenge before you that, once mastered, will open the floodgates of possibilities and unimagined success.

The Subconscious Mind

The subconscious mind is the part of the mind that you typically aren't aware of. It is the work horse performing 95-99% of everything you do as a human being. Think of how much you would have to keep track of if you didn't have your subconscious mind—for example, you'd have to:

- beat your own heart
- remember to breathe
- think about every muscle you needed to move in order to walk
- fight bacteria in your body
- remember to transport blood to every section of your body

We have a subconscious portion of our minds in order to put certain behaviours and thoughts on autopilot so that we have enough space in our conscious mind to think, learn, and grow. The problem is that most people never understand the power of their subconscious mind nor how to deliberately work with it. They have allowed negative behaviours and thoughts to remain on autopilot for so long that they can't imagine doing anything different and this causes them to become stuck.

Your subconscious mind will come to accept and act upon whatever is repeated to it over and over again. This is how you have been conditioned to do the things that society wants you to do.

- You go to University because you have been told so many times that that is what you should do
- You experience a lack of finances because your subconscious mind has been filled with ideas of scarcity since before you were walking
- You get a job, buy a home, and start a family because you've been taught that that's how life works and there are no other options

There's nothing wrong with these experiences if they are what you desire, but therein lies the problem. Most of us go through our entire lives without ever making a clear decision about what we want to do with our life or who we want to be. Thus, we allow our subconscious to control us with the painfully boring default of social conditioning.

You can change your life and paint it as beautifully as you could ever imagine. Want to be a billionaire? You can do it. Want to start a charity that alleviates world hunger? You can do it. It's just that you must first make the decision to do these things and throw all of your efforts into cultivating absolute belief in yourself and your abilities.

2.1.4. You are More than Your Thoughts

The only way that you can begin to recondition your subconscious mind for success is by detaching yourself from the idea that you are your thoughts.

You are not your thoughts.

The vast majority of us think of ourselves as the mental chatter that is constantly going on inside our heads. From this chatter, we have ideas of who we are and what everything around us means. This chatter has been going on since before we can remember so it makes logical sense to assume that this is who we are. The problem with this is that you have to change your thoughts in order to change your life and you may resist the idea of losing your identity.

It is a major threat to our sense of identity to begin altering the conditioning within the subconscious mind. If you have been operating on autopilot for a while your mind and identity have settled into a nice groove and it takes some serious effort to change that groove. It's sort of like how you feel on a cold winter morning while you're nestled in between your warm sheets and cloud-like pillows, the thought of getting out of bed is uncomfortable and doing so requires motivation and will.

Whenever you fully grasp the idea that you are something far greater than your thoughts, beyond words at all, you begin to understand that you do have the power to choose which thoughts you will think.

Try it out:

Think of a purple banana . . . Got it?

Think of a flying elephant . . . Got it?

Think of a green bicycle . . . Got it?

You were able to conjure up images of these incredibly silly ideas because you do have control over your mind. This goes to show you that your mind will do whatever you tell it to do, so altering your subconscious mind and therefore your life is no more difficult a task than telling your mind to do new things.

These new things can be described of places of complete belief in yourself and your abilities regardless of what anyone else thinks or says. The people all around you have practiced thoughts of unbelief in themselves for so long that they can't even imagine how someone could actually believe in themselves. This will most certainly cause some turmoil as you begin to change your mind as these individuals whom you are surrounded by will feel threatened by your disembarking of the normal path. The socially acceptable path is one of disbelief in one's self and you have got to summon the strength to go against the grain and begin to believe in yourself.

A simple way to grasp this idea of the mind and thoughts is to compare it to a computer. Your subconscious mind can be compared to the hard drive, the actual machine itself; your conscious mind can be compared to the programs that are loaded on the machine, and you can be compared to the programmer, who chooses the programs that are installed on the computer. Your thoughts and beliefs are nothing but programs that are installed on your hard-drive and since they determine the course of your life it would be wise to install the most beneficial programs you can find! All it takes to reprogram your mind is a sincere desire to do so and an indomitable persistence to stick with it day after day.

2.1.5. The Importance of Thinking

It has been said before that the only thing that makes a man a man at all is his mind, the rest can be found in a pig or a horse. Thinking is the highest function of which man is capable and yet so few of us take the time to exercise this magnificent gift.

The majority of us operate just like animals which isn't intended to be offensive but intended to reveal truth. We go through our day to day activities on autopilot reacting to stimuli in our environment. 95 percent of us will go through our entire lives without ever actually thinking once! This is kind of hard to believe but take a look at your own life, when was the last time you actually sat down and put your mind to use to find a creative solution to a particular problem? Probably never and you're not alone.

We must not make the mistake of assuming that mental chatter is thinking. Remembering to feed your dog or finish an assignment isn't thinking, and reacting to stimuli around you isn't thinking. Thinking is the process of actively engaging the full capabilities of the mind in order to devise a possible solution to a specific problem. If we would simply think, many of our problems could be solved in a very short amount of time; instead, we are content to run on autopilot and complain about our problems which does nothing.

We also must not make the mistake of assuming that since one is intelligent, he or she is thinking. You can learn and memorize all of the books in the world but that still isn't thinking as no intelligent action will come from it. Without thought, intelligence is like a stagnant pond with nowhere to flow, it does nothing and eventually evaporates as what isn't in motion is eventually lost.

The reason so few of us ever put our marvelous minds to work is that we were never taught how to think. We go through our entire academic career and not once do we take 'Thinking 101' or 'Reasoning 102'. We are taught subject after subject and from this we are expected to learn how to think; some do learn to think through this method, but most of us don't.

Thinking is a skill that can be learned and mastered just like shooting a basketball. The most successful individuals are those that have learned how to think creatively upon their problems. The top performers that we've already talked about aren't people without problems, they often have the same problems as every single one of us, the difference is that they have learned how to use their marvelous mind to solve those problems.

It's fairly easy to realize the stupendous benefits of learning how to think. If you would take but one hour a day and creatively think about how you can do better, your life would become one of joy and beauty. Your mind can be likened to a gold mine wherein it only takes the willingness to dig to find the golden nuggets that can completely change your life.

2.1.6. The Power of Focus

The power to focus is one of the most important abilities of the mind. A poorly developed ability to focus will cause life to be difficult and many tasks will seem impossible; on the flip side, a properly developed ability to focus causes distractions to become almost nonexistent and tasks become effortless as you dive in and complete one after the other.

In your brain lies a peculiar mechanism called the 'Reticular Activating System', or *'RAS'* for short. This brilliant little system allows you to filter the immense amount of data constantly flooding into your brain in order to find what's important to you. Without a RAS you would be completely overwhelmed by the data you would have to process just to live your day to day life. Your RAS learns your habits of focus and from that information it filters all of the data that comes your way on a moment to moment basis.

In simpler terms, this means that **you will only ever find what you're looking for.**

Your habitual point of focus can be likened to a pair of glasses with a coloured lens. Whenever you put the glasses on, everything you see is tinted with the colour of the lens. In the same way, whatever you spend your time focusing on will determine the colour and texture that your life takes on. This is another very important reason to give your sincere efforts to cultivating a positive, happy mindset. The more that you decide to focus upon good feeling things, the more these good feeling things will show up in your environment by the way of your RAS.

Your point of focus also determines the thoughts that occupy your mind. Inevitably, if you begin to focus upon thoughts of your feet, these thoughts will begin flowing into your mind and so on with any other subject. Your focus can be likened to a direct command given to your mind that tells it what to think about next and it's important that we give the commands that lead to a better life.

If you choose to focus upon reasons for why you can achieve your goals and dreams, you will find them; likewise, if you choose to focus upon reasons for why you can't achieve your goals, then you will find those also. **It really is as simple as looking for what you want to see.**

A great number of us go through our lives feeling doomed by so called "bad luck". Understand that there is nothing superstitious or mysterious about how the Universe operates; it plays no games, has no favourites, and operates according to set law which it advertises in every blade of grass and every star in the sky. The most successful individuals to ever walk this planet were those that made earnest study of these laws and lived their lives in accordance with them.

"Bad luck" only happens to a person because that is what he or she is focused upon. They think that it is just who they are and that they are doomed to poverty and failure. Inevitably, this focus can bring nothing but poverty and failure to their life! Whenever you see anybody failing at life you can be sure that the problem is thoughts of failure; on the other hand, whenever you see anybody succeeding in life you can be absolutely positive that their thoughts are those of success and well-being.

Your thoughts create your reality and your thoughts are determined by your point of focus. Begin today to focus upon only that which you want to see such as happiness, love, connectedness, ease, success, etc. and your life will begin to change at once.

2.2

CHAPTER 4: ATTITUDE

2.2.1. Introduction

Your attitude can be defined as your habitual way of perceiving and relating to the world around you. When we talk about the marvelous abilities of the mind, the ability to choose your attitude is certainly one of the most impressive. We have the ability to consciously decide how we will relate to the world around us; we can relate in a generally positive manner or a generally negative manner. The majority of society operates with a reactive attitude. This means that they mirror what is being presented to them in their reality; if something pleasant occurs they are happy, but if something negative occurs they are frustrated. These people allow their attitudes to be determined by circumstances outside of their control and act as a passenger to life instead of the driver that they could be.

If you are to achieve your own big ideas, you must consciously *choose* the attitude that you carry out into the world. Without choosing your attitude you will be thrown about by every circumstance presented to you, much like a ship at sea without a rudder. If you allow yourself to react to life you will be forever chained to the status quo; however, by choosing your attitude you allow yourself to glide easily from one accomplishment to the next for the rest of your life.

2.2.2. The Key to Successful Living

Your attitude towards life determines life's attitude towards you. When you begin to control how you perceive your reality you gain the ability to change it in any way you see fit. By maintaining a positive attitude life presents you with predominantly positive experiences, and this is the basis of positive psychology.

A good attitude is the key to not only success, but also to good luck. Those who have poor attitudes often use the word 'luck' in order to excuse themselves from taking control of their own minds and explain their current life situation. As you begin to cultivate a happier, more positive outlook on life you'll be surprised at the abundance of fresh opportunities that will continually flood into your experience.

As you roll out of bed in the morning and shut off your alarm clock, you choose what attitude you will carry out into the world that day. This choice is often made unconsciously as we continue the patterns of the past but we do have the ability to make this choice consciously. You can choose to be happy and expect great things every single day! The realisation that expectations are a choice was a huge breakthrough for myself. I finally understood that I could expect the best from life without having to justify that expectation, and as I moved in this direction my reality actually began to change. I went from expecting and living negative events to expecting and living positive events, but the change had to first occur at the level of expectation.

Your attitude is something that can be trained just like the muscles of your body. A good strategy is the 'fake it until you make it' approach wherein you simply act like you are happy and act like you expect positive things. If you stick with it long enough, you'll begin to actually adopt these new attitudes as your own and your whole life experience will begin to change.

Attitudes are contagious, much like a nasty virus. Take a look at your circle of friends and if you're honest with yourself you'll see that your entire group generally adopts the same outlook and expectations toward life. There may be a variety of different personalities within your circle of friends, but the outlook on life tends to be very similar. The more time you spend with someone the more your attitudes begin to resemble one another. This is where we come to the conclusion that you become who you hang out with. Your five closest friends will give you an accurate snapshot of the dominant attitude that you carry.

Honestly answer these questions to get a better idea of who you are becoming by your association with your friends:

- How happy are my friends?
- What do they expect out of life?
- Do they expect to be successful?
- Do they expect financial scarcity?
- Do they have positive relationships in their lives?
- Do they have goals that they are committed to achieving?
- Do they put in serious efforts to become better people on a daily basis?

- Are they fit or overweight and out of shape?
- Do they party often and use drugs?

Answering these questions honestly can be tough as it's uncomfortable to face truth in the eye. Understand that you will become your closest acquaintances, there is no getting around this fact of life. If you don't like your answers to the questions above then that tells you something about yourself and the next step you need to take in your life. You must disconnect with the friends that you don't want to be like and seek out friends that have the same qualities as who you wish to become.

This is a well-known phenomenon by the top performers, and this is why you see them only hanging out with other high achievers. They understand that who they spend their time with has a huge effect on their mindset, their attitude, and their ability to achieve their dreams.

You can alter your own attitude by consciously choosing to do so. After you make this choice you'll find that new opportunities and circumstances quickly appear in your reality. It's as if the Universe is acknowledging your willingness to change by bringing you anything that will help smooth out the transition period.

Begin today to cultivate an attitude of joy, success, and well-being. This not only affects you but it affects every person that you come into contact with. You become a beacon of high-flying, positive energy in the stormy seas of negative attitudes that are so common today in our society. An excellent attitude is your greatest gift to the world.

2.2.3. How to Build Mental Strength

Since you now know that your attitude is something that can be developed like the muscles of your body, how do you do it? How do you go about developing a specific mindset toward life that will increase your happiness and success?

Mental strength is the ability to think and feel how you choose to in any given moment. For example, you're driving down the road and somebody cuts you off; with sufficient mental strength, you won't allow yourself to get frustrated or angry. Or let's say that someone close to you begins to criticise your decisions in life; with sufficient mental strength you can stand in the clarity of your decision and not allow this other person to affect your confidence.

You can see how critical a skill like this is for successful living. It takes a lot of strength to live congruently with your highest ideas in the face of a society that values conformity above everything else. It takes strength to allow criticism and hate to roll right off of you like water off a turtle's shell. As you pursue your dreams there will be no shortage of people around you criticising you. They'll ask who you are to think you can achieve such grand things, they'll tell you that it's impossible; they'll tell you that it's a pipe dream and you should just give up before you fail miserably. These types of comments become more and more common the farther you follow your own path.

It takes mental strength not to take things personally.

Have you noticed that when you allow things to get to you, the momentum of negativity builds until you totally feel like crap? The more inclined you are to be affected by what goes on around you, the more you are at the whim of your environment and the less able you are to direct the course of your life.

A key component to mental strength is focus which is the ability to direct your mind. When you develop your focus you give yourself the freedom of venturing out into the unknown by understanding that you can always find the positive in any situation.

The first step towards developing mental strength is becoming aware of when you are mentally weak. Begin to watch yourself as if from an outsider's point of view. Notice when you react to what life throws your way, and notice when you allow the circumstances in your environment to affect how you feel. As you begin to become more aware of when you are mentally weak your desire for mental strength will increase tremendously.

After you understand where you're weak mentally it's time to begin training up. The best way that I have found to do this is through the process of meditation. I know what you are thinking—monks in red robes with shaved heads that levitate—this level of mediation is not at all what I am talking about. Meditation enables the detached outsider's perspective and develops focus to an unbelievable degree. The specifics of meditation will be discussed in a later chapter as it couldn't possibly be left out of this book.

All in all, the desire to improve your mental strength will lead you towards the path of its development. Most things in life are like that wherein all you need is a desire and commitment and the rest will unfold beautifully before you. Remember, the mind is a wonderful servant, but a terrible master; you must take control of your mind or it will take control of you.

2.2.4. Consume Positive Messages

The quality of output in your life, whether it be your thoughts, your attitude, or your creativity, is largely determined by the quality of input. Consuming positive messages of success and excellence will produce acts of success and excellence if given enough time; on the flip side, consuming negative messages of fear and insecurity will produce fearful actions.

Begin to become aware of what you allow into your mind. By necessity, your mind accepts and adopts the flavour of whatever you habitually consume. Your mind is like a sponge, it absorbs all the information you expose it too. We are constantly bombarded by advertisements and other messages of fear and insecurity in order that we may be more easily controlled. You watch t.v., listen to radio, and while it may not seem like it does much, after you watch it continuously the messages of the advertisers and t.v. programmers begin to subtly influence how you act. You begin to spend money impulsively, act like your favourite characters, and much more. These forms of entertainment are not 'bad' but it is important to realize that they will influence your mind, so be very picky about what you allow in.

If you have not made the conscious choice to consume positive messages then you are, by default, consuming negative messages. There is an abundance of negativity that surrounds each and every one of us whether we like it or not. Turn on the news and see how you feel after watching fearful messages minute after fearful minute.

Turn on popular music and see how you feel after hearing about heartbreak and depression. The point is that you must filter out the negativity from your life if you are to grow at the rate at which you are capable.

Consuming personal development material is an excellent way to cultivate a successful mindset. The people that create these programs are very successful themselves and by listening to them day after day you are literally adopting their mindsets by osmosis. Just like we talked about earlier when we discussed how you become who you hang out with, by listening to these programs you are 'hanging out' with these ultra-successful people and this has massively positive effects on your own life.

Some other examples of positive material are:

- Seminars
- Audio books

    o Great for listening in your car or during mundane activities

- Books
- Uplifting music
- Upbeat acquaintances
- A positive group of people that are committed to developing themselves and achieving great things

I don't expect you to blindly accept any of the ideas or advice in this book. I want you to take these ideas and put them to the test in your own life so you can then make your own decisions. Direct experience with these ideas will be of much more value than simply reading about them. Put this section to the test in your life by committing thirty days to listening, reading, or otherwise consuming positive messages for at least 1 hour a day. If you perform this experiment in your own life, I am sure that you will be pleasantly surprised by differences you see in your habitual attitudes. You'll start believing in yourself, your dreams, and you'll begin to carry an attitude of well-being with you wherever you go.

I have created a rolodex of some excellent sources of positive messages so you have plenty of options to perform your thirty day test. Read through the list and find what draws your attention and get going, you won't regret it. You can find the resources here: http://carlaschesser.com.au/resources/

2.2.5. Self-Confidence

Confidence in yourself is absolutely critical to living a joyful life. If you don't trust yourself you will find people and things to place your trust in and you'll slowly give away your power. You'll notice that the happiest people you meet are those that are truly confident in themselves and their abilities. They know themselves, their strengths, their weaknesses, and they accept it all fully and completely. They aren't trying to be something that they are not.

Society wants you to believe that self-confidence is something that comes from the approval others. This is why you see so many people attempting to gain self-confidence by hitting the gym everyday (for vanity purposes not health reasons), trying to look as cool as they can, and many other silly games. They are seeking their validation in the approval of others and so they run in circles trying to please person after person in hopes that they will one day feel like they are enough.

If society can succeed in convincing you that your confidence lies in the approval of others you are more easily controlled. You can see this is as clear as night and day when you look at advertisements on t.v. Almost every single one is attempting to sell you something by showing you how cool and accepted you'll be after you buy their product. They manipulate you based on your fears of being alone in order to make a quick buck.

If you only feel good about yourself whenever you have been accepted and approved of by another individual, you can never be free. With this mindset you will always be a slave to your ideas of what you *should* do and who you *should* be and you never truly get in touch with yourself.

The path to true happiness lies in self-acceptance and self-validation. What you might normally consider confidence is nothing but a false bravado used to mask hidden anxieties and fears. True confidence isn't a puffed out chest and a *too cool for school* attitude. It is the complete acceptance of oneself, faults and all.

When you release the idea of trying to become who you *should* be as dictated by society, your parents, your friends, and so on, you gain a new sense of freedom. You stop running around in circles trying to please everybody and for the first time you don't care what anyone else thinks. This is an absolutely beautiful state of mind to be in as you finally start to follow your own ideas and become who you were meant to be instead of fitting into the mould everyone else has for you.

As corny as it sounds, human beings are like snowflakes where no two of us are even remotely alike (I told you it was going to sound corny!). We each have a unique blend of strengths, talents, weaknesses, characteristics, life experiences, and so forth. We are each so different from one another that it would be incredibly foolish to try and be like anybody else. We are each our own geniuses and we must identify this genius and develop it if we are to ever be fully fulfilled.

Ralph Waldo Emerson once said, "There comes a point in every man's life when he realizes that envy is ignorance, and imitation is suicide." Think about that for a second . . . What a marvelous quote that is! Jealousy is ignorant because we each have our own individual strengths and to wish you had someone else's strengths is silly. Imitation is suicide because by trying to be somebody else you kill your true self in the process.

You are a unique and talented individual with an extraordinary amount of 'you' qualities. Look inside yourself and try and identify where you might cultivate your own form of genius. Stop trying to be like your favourite celebrity or the cool kid at the party. Take some time with a journal and a pen and begin searching for your true self. Who are you and what can you become? Find where you could excel if you tried and you will find your true calling, your heart's path.

True happiness lies in the realization that you yourself are enough. Your acceptance is the only acceptance you will ever need and nobody else's opinion really matters. Recognize your genius and do your best to share it with the world. All advancement of any kind has always depended upon an individual sharing his unique genius in a way that we could benefit from. It is selfish of you to hold your true self back in order to blend in. Your responsibility is that of shining your light as bright as you can and showing by example that it's okay for others to do the same.

To summarize this entire section I want to share a quote from Marianne Williamson. It's honestly the best quote I've ever come across as it so accurately describes how most of us are living our lives today:

"Our deepest fear is not that we are inadequate. Our deepest fear is that we are powerful beyond measure. It is our light, not our darkness that most frightens us. We ask ourselves, 'Who am I to be brilliant, gorgeous, talented, fabulous?' Actually, who are you not to be? You are a child of God. Your playing small does not serve the world. There is nothing enlightened about shrinking so that other people won't feel insecure around you. We are all meant to shine, as children do. We were born to make manifest the glory of God that is within us. It's not just in some of us; it's in everyone. And as we let our own light shine, we unconsciously give other people permission to do the same. As we are liberated from our own fear, our presence automatically liberates others."

2.3

CHAPTER 5:
HEALTH FIRST, WEALTH LATER

2.3.1. Introduction

If I were to pick one area of my life to master before tackling any other area, that area would be health. Physical wellbeing is the most important aspect of successful living. You literally can't enjoy anything you accomplish without feeling good enough physically to enjoy it! If you have aches and pains or are lethargic because you're overweight, no amount of money or success will help you feel any better.

The good thing is that outstanding levels of health and fitness can be enjoyed by installing a few new habits into your everyday life. It's important to realize that health won't come to you overnight and that there is no short cut or magic pill that will solve all of your problems.

Excellent health is a lifetime process and it's a lifestyle choice that you make every single day. You can't work your butt off, get yourself into great shape, and then stop exercising proclaiming your success. Your body doesn't care what you did six months ago or even two months ago, its mantra is "what have you done for me lately?".

Mastering your health is certainly not easy but I promise that it will get easier with time. It's never easy to start a new habit and especially one that requires such immense levels of exertion. Stick with it however and you'll find that you start to really enjoy both exercise and eating healthy. There is immense satisfaction to be enjoyed from taking proper care of yourself. Getting into shape is one of the quickest ways to boost your self-esteem and outlook on life, not to mention a myriad of other benefits.

Focus on your health and you'll have all the energy necessary to achieve the lofty dreams that you have for your life.

2.3.2. Your Health is Huge

Think about the people that you are surrounded by as you move throughout your day. Notice just how many people there are that are overweight and out of shape. The majority of people treat their bodies like they are invincible and that their poor habits won't really make a difference. They eat fried fake foods and lead sedentary lives with the majority of their exercise consisting of walking to and from their car everyday.

These are the patterns that you will fall into if you don't take the time to personally master this area of your life. Achieving great health requires going against the grain and this is just another difficulty on top of the already difficult physical exertion.

I present you these ideas to paint an accurate picture in your mind so you are adequately prepared when you do decide to master your health. I know that by setting your expectations straight you'll be less likely to quit when the going gets tough. You must realize that mastering your health requires persistence, effort, and a sincere desire to do so. A weak hope of better health will never get you to where you wish to go.

Your natural state of being is one of exuberant health and vibrant energy. We would all be incredibly healthy if we would only stop doing the things that make us unhealthy.

Advertisers pay millions of dollars every year to convince you that your body is weak and that tiny germs can make you sick for days on end. This isn't true. Your body has a brilliant in-house defense system capable of fending off even the worst viruses. It is only our belief in weak bodies that creates weak bodies.

Our sedentary lifestyles and obsession with instant gratification is leading us towards miserable existences of laziness and apathy. We are a collective whole and the health of the whole depends upon the health the individual. If we continue our current trends we are not going to be in a pretty place in the years to come and the damage may be irreversible.

You may be incredibly out of shape or just average, but it doesn't really matter where you currently stand. The work is the same and the lifestyle choices are the same, it may just take you longer to see the results that you want. Many people resist the work required to get into shape and this is because they project the future into their now experience. They think about all of the exercise they have to do and they allow themselves to feel overwhelmed by the idea of it. In essence, they're trying to work out on days that haven't even arrived yet! Forget this perspective and take it one day at a time. Each day you exercise is one day closer to a vibrant state of being that will change your life for the better.

It's important that you take an honest look at your current habits regarding health and fitness.

- How are you doing so far?
- Are you overweight?
- Do you eat junk food regularly?
- How often do you exercise?
- Where do you predict your state of health will be five years from now? Ten? Thirty?
- Are your habits leading you towards a life of energy and vibrancy? Or towards a life of laziness and lethargy?
- Could you do better if you really wanted to?
- Do you want to be healthier than you now are?
- How healthy do you desire to be?

Answering these questions may be tough but it's crucial that you see the truth for what it is.

Your health habits not only affect your quality of life but they also greatly affect the lives of those around you. What kind of example are you setting for the people in your life? If you had kids would you want them to adopt your current habits?

Our actions will always affect more than just us. We are a connected whole and what we do at the individual level ultimately affects every single person on this planet either directly or indirectly. What kind of a planet are you creating? What kind of a planet do you want to create?

2.3.3. Healthy Eating for a Healthy Life

Your nutrition is the most important factor when it comes to realising and maintaining a healthy body, mind, and life. The old saying "you are what you eat" is a fairly accurate statement. If you desire vibrant energy and feelings of aliveness then you have to eat foods that are of that quality. Does a bag of cookies scream energy and aliveness? Or does it scream sluggish and bloated?

As a species, we eat way more food than is actually needed to survive. This is readily apparent whenever you stop and observe the state of health of the average individual. The human body doesn't need much food to survive, and when you continually feed it more than it needs it stores the excess as fat. This eventually clogs your body with junk and decreases the quality of your life. If you often feel lethargic and unmotivated the likely culprit is your diet.

Eating healthy isn't as difficult as most people make it out to be. There are a staggering amount of new diets that hit the market every year, each one claiming to be the latest and greatest thing since sliced bread. But I'm going to dash your hopes right now, no new fad diet will ever be the magic bullet solution to your health problems.

The easiest way to correct your diet is by tuning in to your intuition. Ask yourself before every meal if the food you are about to consume is going to contribute to your life or contribute to disease, and then listen and follow your honest expectation. If you'll ask this question before every meal for just one short month I promise you that you will never look at food the same. If you can maintain this for a month, and be completely honest with yourself, you'll develop a habit that will serve you for the rest of your life.

We intuitively know what is healthy but we often ignore our intuition in order to comfort ourselves with unhealthy food. This results in the habit of eating when one isn't even physically hungry. They are emotionally hungry; hungry for satisfaction with life and lasting fulfilment. This is a hunger that can never be satisfied by food no matter how delicious it may be.

Over time, we have evolved to this day in age where we barely have to lift a finger in order to secure a meal. You can drive down almost any road and have ten or fifteen options of delicious food to choose from. This is both a blessing and a curse as it must be coupled with the self-discipline to consume in moderation, and this often isn't the case. When this self-discipline isn't present, the result is the obesity epidemic that we're currently experiencing.

The most optimal diet for human beings is one that heavily incorporates fruits and vegetables. Consuming anything that is grown fresh from the ground is an excellent way to increase your energy, happiness, and ultimately, your chances for success in life. If you want to be lively then you must increase your consumption of foods that are lively as you decrease your consumption of foods that are dead.

Another incredibly important aspect of a healthy diet is proper hydration. Our bodies are about 60% water which makes it obvious just how critical it is to proper health. Without adequate hydration our bodies cannot function at optimal levels and all of its processes are slowed down tremendously; however, with proper hydration we experience abundant energy and the maintenance of a healthy weight. If you want to know if you need to drink more water pay attention the next time you go to the restroom. If your urine is a dark yellowish-gold then you are dehydrated. The optimal state of hydration results in near clear urine which lets you know that enough water is in your system to properly dispose of any harmful toxins.

Unfortunately, eating a healthy diet requires going against the grain. The majority of food that surrounds us is primarily processed. This means that the food is fake and holds no real nutritional value for your body. They are basically empty calories with sugar on top to make them taste good, and that's why the majority of us indulge! However, there is something that is much more delicious than the instant satisfaction of a sweet roll and that's a satisfaction with the choices we make on a daily basis. There is no greater feeling than knowing without a doubt that you are doing what's best for your body and health.

Eating unhealthy is a choice regardless of whether you make it consciously or unconsciously. Whenever you choose to eat an unhealthy meal you are choosing disease and decay. There is no getting around this and there is no denying this. You can try to lie to yourself and those around you, but in the end you are the one that suffers. Better to face up to the truth of your current eating habits before they get any worse. Your challenges with your diet or any area of your life aren't going to go away on their own. Denial is one of the worst strategies to deal with your problems.

Begin treating your body with the respect that you would treat someone who you deeply admired. Your body works day and night to keep you healthy and alive and it's disrespectful to feed it the processed food that a lot of us do. Your body enables you to move around and provides you the energy necessary to make all of your dreams come true. It does all this and so much more and asks for nothing except that you provide it the proper fuel.

General Nutrition Tips

- Begin to eat smaller meals (more like snacks) spread throughout your day. Aim for 5-6 of these small meals every 2-3 hours in order to continually provide your body nutrients and stabilise your energy and emotions
- Hydrate! Drink more water than you think you need to and you'll begin noticing a difference in how you feel in less than a week
- Start cutting back on eating out. There are virtually no fast food restaurants that offer truly healthy meals even though they may advertise some meals as such. Replace eating out with eating a nice home cooked meal. You'll benefit your body and save money
- Consult your intuition and ask yourself if what you're about to eat is adding to or taking away from your life

- Eliminate processed sugars, trans-fats, high fructose corn syrup, and low quality calories from your diet. These only taste good for a second but then your body has to struggle to digest them for hours

- Consume high quality calories from more natural foods (fruits, veggies, whole grains, lean meat, dairy, etc.)

- Whenever you feel like eating for emotional reasons, get out a journal and actually listen to what your emotions are telling you about your life. Working through your emotions instead of distracting yourself from them with food is a much wiser strategy in the long run

- Replace your desire for sweets with a desire for natural sweets such as bananas, mangoes, and other delicious fruits

- Clean out your pantry and refrigerator of all foods that hold you back from becoming the best you

- Cook healthy meals a week in advance so that you always have quick access to a nutritious meal

- Buy and study a number of books on proper nutrition so that you have the knowledge required to make educated decisions

- Recruit a friend and the both of you start challenging each other to make healthier and

healthier choices with your diet. Having a friend for support is a great way to adhere to a new habit
- Join a cooking class to learn how to cook delicious and nutritious meals
- Find foods that are both tasty and nutritious! I promise you there are **plenty**!

2.3.4. Get Moving

Physical exercise is one of the greatest things you can ever do for your body. The benefits are stupendous and it is so incredibly worth the effort that it requires. Some of the benefits include:

- Increased motivation
- Increased energy
- Increased self-confidence and self-esteem
- Increased sex drive
- Increased happiness
- A clearer, more efficient mind
- Stress relief
- Increased feelings of well-being
- Stronger immune system
- Increased productivity
- Increased social activity

If the thought of exercise doesn't do much for you, you're not alone. There are countless millions of people that cringe at the idea of physical exertion and in the end they suffer for it.

There really isn't an option when it comes to physical exercise. Technically you do have an option but the decision is a no-brainer:

1. Exercise on a daily basis and continually improve the quality of your life, or
2. Don't exercise and allow the quality of your life to decline year after year

The way I see it, the choice is clear; how about you?

Perhaps the most outstanding benefit of physical exercise is that it literally makes you more intelligent. It does this by stimulating the growth of new brain cells and reducing the stress that kills brain cells. At this point in your life I'm sure you can see that the smarter you become, the better off you will be.

The most common obstacle to consistent physical exercise is the insidious *something for nothing* mindset. This mindset believes that worthwhile results can be achieved for little or no effort. This is the most destructive mindset that you could ever carry with you in life. The simple fact is, **nothing worthwhile can be achieved without first paying the price.**

There is no industry that reveals our urge for instant gratification more than the health and fitness industry. Turn on the television for more than a few minutes and you're bound to see a commercial pitching the *latest* and *greatest* exercise machine or fat burning pill that can get you the body of your dreams for four easy payments of $19.99. These advertisers know that you want to be in shape, they know that you don't want to put in the effort, and they know that you want a fit body now. They manipulate you in order to make a profit.

The truth is, the only way to achieve a fit body and vibrant health is by consistently exercising day after day, week after week. That's it. As a rule of thumb, if it sounds too good to be true, it is. Leave it at that and instead get your butt off the couch and hit the gym.

Fortunately, it doesn't take too long to start seeing the results of your exercise efforts. If you will commit yourself to intense exercise at least five times a week, every week, for three months you will start to see results. In my experience, three months seems to be the time wherein your body begins to respond to the increase in physical movement. As soon as you start to see your body change you'll be hooked and you'll never look back. All it takes is the determination to stick with it during the initial months and your life will never be the same.

Daily exercise in combination with proper eating is the recipe for a long and energetic life. You will feel incredible about yourself, your life, and things will continue to get better and better for you. I understand that it is difficult to start these new habits and I understand that the work isn't easy, but I also understand the results of these habits. Once you experience the benefits of a few months of consistent exercise you will want to go back in time and give yourself a hug for sticking with it.

The most effective form of exercise is what's called aerobic exercise or cardio. This is exercise that aims to elevate your heart rate for a certain duration of time. Your elevated heart rate pumps blood throughout your body at an increased rate which delivers more oxygen and nutrients to every part. This type of exercise also challenges your body and as a result increases the efficiency at which it operates, which means a longer life!

If you're just starting out with exercise, take it slow and progress your way up. You can't fix your health overnight, it takes consistent effort. It's better to *actually* exercise twice a week than merely *think* about exercising five times. Do what you can and slowly increase the amount as you grow stronger. Begin by performing just three sessions of aerobic exercise per week at a duration of at least twenty minutes. Once you have established this habit it will be much easier to accomplish more.

Some excellent forms of aerobic exercise are jumping rope, jogging, power walking, rowing, and anything else that really gets your body moving and your heart pumping.

There's no need to make this complicated. Start small and simple and before you know it you'll experience dramatic changes in your body and feelings. As you progress you can learn absolutely everything you need to know from the internet. There are a ton of free websites that can help you along your new path towards a better, healthier future.

General Physical Exercise Tips

- Start slow and work your way up. It doesn't matter how slow you go as long as you never stop moving
- Allow your body to get plenty of rest after exercise so your muscles can recover and grow
- Feed your body healthy foods within forty five minutes of exercise as this is the time when your body needs proper nutrition the most
- Sign up for a group class at your local gym. Having others around to exercise with makes the process a lot easier

- Recruit a buddy and both of you start an exercise program. Hold each other accountable and really commit to continuing with the program. A buddy makes exercise more fun and will increase your probabilities of sticking out the tough first months

- Do whatever it takes to exercise consistently for the first 3 months. Growl, yell, and scream if you have to, but get that exercise session in! You'll be glad you did

- Look to the long term and realise that intelligent action today (exercise) will yield phenomenal results

- Sign up for personal training sessions at your local gym in order to learn how to exercise properly and be held accountable for your progress

- Motivate yourself by cutting out pictures of bodies that inspire you to get out and get moving

- Exercise at least three times a week, ideally five

- Pick a set time to exercise and stick with it! You're much more likely to exercise if you say, "every Monday, Wednesday, and Friday I work out for thirty minutes at 5:30 p.m."", versus, "yeah I'll try and work out three times this week!". Make your plans concrete

- Put exercise reminders in your phone calendar so that you never conveniently "forget"

- Bet a friend or family member that you'll work out three days a week for the next three months. This will hold you accountable as you won't want to embarrass yourself

- Find exercise that you thoroughly enjoy or that you could very much enjoy once you get really good at it. Choosing exercise that you find fun is a great way to stay committed. Some examples are rock climbing, hiking, jogging with friends, or rowing

- Overall, learn to enjoy the journey! You'll never be finished and so you better learn to enjoy yourself as you move towards greater and greater health

2.4

CHAPTER 6:
GOALS

2.4.1. Introduction

Goals are one of those necessary things for living a successful life. The vast majority of people never set goals, and if you were to ask someone what they were working towards they would most likely answer with vagueness. Without goals you don't know where you're going, and this lack of control creates tremendous anxiety within.

Goals allow you to yield greater control over your own life experience, or at least allow you to feel like you do. You do possess the ability to set any goal that you would like to achieve and eventually succeed if you remain committed.

Therein lies the secret to achieving anything you want in life, commitment.

Schools and universities alike leave out the course 'Goals 101' so it is up to us as individuals to learn how to set and achieve effective goals. The high achievers that we keep returning to almost always have goals that they are working towards. As soon as they achieve one they celebrate momentarily and then set an even higher plateau towards which to climb. Setting and achieving goals is a lifetime endeavor that allows us to enjoy the thrill of the chase.

2.4.2. The Real Purpose of Goals

There's a lot of different advice on goal setting around the personal development field. Most of it is generally the same and it revolves around the premise of identifying what you would like to achieve, have, or do at some point in the future. This seems to be a logical approach to setting goals, I mean isn't that what goals are? Something that you want to bring about in your life?

While the above thought process may seem logical, in fact, it is an inferior way to go about setting goals. This goal setting method is based upon a false belief in the reality of time. Let's break that down.

Time is a man-made invention which serves the purpose of increasing order in our lives. Time does not actually exist somewhere *out there.* As George Carlin said, there are no numbers in the sky as nature does not keep time. You never see animals pull out a pocket watch to see how long they have before they're late. Time only exists in our minds. The Universe operates on one time only, and that time is the **now**.

The now is the present moment. This moment and this moment and this moment and so on ad infinitum. All you have ever had, all you ever have, and all you ever will have is the present moment. I hear your objections, you say, "the past most certainly does exist! I can remember just the way it was". This objection may seem valid but let's think about it, whenever you remember the 'past' you are doing so in the present moment. The same goes for imagining the future. You are always in the present moment and you can enjoy it fully, think about the past, or attempt to predict the future. The choice is yours.

If you try to set goals based upon the idea that time actually exists, you diminish your enjoyment of the entire journey. You live for some future moment and cease enjoying your *now* experience.

The real purpose of goals is to sharpen your present moment focus and improve the quality of your life **now**. Whenever you contemplate a goal that you want to achieve, are you filled with passion, excitement, and enthusiasm at the very thought of it? If you answered yes then that particular goal has improved the quality of your life right now and is therefore a keeper. If your goal doesn't make you feel incredible by just thinking about it, you need to drop it. It isn't worthy of your attention.

Another common model for goal setting is the S.M.A.R.T model. This model says that your goals should be specific, measurable, attainable, realistic, and time bound. This model can most certainly work and it does work for a lot of people, but your goals do not have to be this specific.

The primary aim of your goal is to bring clarity to your daily decisions and a more general goal possesses the ability to do this.

- Should you hit the gym or go see a movie with your friends?
- Should you go to the library and check out some books or go on a date?
- Should you sleep in or get up early and get a head start on your day?
- Should you apply for a job or start your own business?

None of these options are better than the other, but your answer will depend solely on what goals that you have set for yourself.

If you don't have any goals for yourself you'll drift through life without wielding any control over your direction. You have no basis for making your decisions and so you'll typically accept the status quo and not do much to change it. Once you set and achieve a goal for yourself I think you'll find your life much more satisfying as you'll enjoy a much greater sense of clarity.

It has been shown repeatedly that a person's satisfaction with life is based directly upon how much control they feel they have. Without goals, you feel out of control and you allow other's ideas to become your own without a second thought. With goals, you gain a feeling of control as you glide from one achievement to the next as you sculpt your life exactly as you'd like it to be.

With this new understanding of setting goals that improve the quality of your life now, it's important that you identify what goals that **you** would like to achieve. Whenever you first begin setting goals you'll most likely set goals that aren't yours but that are society's goals for you. You'll probably set a goal to earn a certain amount of money, to buy a certain car, or to live in a mansion. Nothing is wrong with these goals whatsoever if this is what you <u>truly</u> want, but often this isn't actually what you want.

It takes time to cut through social conditioning and find out what is really wanted from life. You've got to take the time to be alone and do some soul searching in order to identify what you really would like to achieve. There is no 'right' and 'wrong' for goals, the only 'right' is that you select a goal that resonates with your highest self.

This, in its essence, is defining your own idea of success.

There is one more model of goal setting that I want to present to you before we move on. In this model, you set and pursue goals that are in alignment with the character aspects of yourself. There may be a part of you that really likes to push yourself to become better and better and achieve great things. There may be another part of you that really enjoys being a part of community and helping those around you. There may be another part of you that loves to soak up new information and constantly learn new ideas and skills.

Instead of setting goals based upon what you would like to achieve, you set goals based upon the development of these different parts of you. Going along with the above example, perhaps you would set a goal to start and build a community of individuals that is dedicated to learning and growing in a particular field. This goal would incorporate all of those aspects and would therefore be an expression of yourself instead of something outside of yourself that you wish to achieve.

This causes your goal to be much more intrinsically motivating and you're much more likely to stay committed. With this model, you work to develop your strengths and your character in order to more fully express yourself to the world.

2.4.3. How to Set Effective Goals

There are two ways to set goals:

1) With your head, and
2) With your heart.

The most common method is to use logic to set goals while giving little, if any, consideration to the heart component. This is a recipe for failure as your logic alone cannot keep you committed to your goal in the face of adversity. Goals that satisfy both the mind and the heart will be the goals that keep you committed until achievement.

The problem is that it's difficult to listen to what our hearts have to say. We continually consume stimulants that quiet the opinions of the heart in favour of the logic. I'm talking particularly about caffeine and alcohol. These substances throw your body's natural intelligence out of whack and you fall out of sync with your true self. You start living a life that you don't want to live and using these substances to push yourself farther down the path.

The only way to find out what both your mind and heart want is to stop consuming the substances that prevent this coherence from naturally taking place. This means that for a week do not consume anything unnatural; no caffeine, no alcohol, no other drugs, etc. This week will detox your body and sync your mind and heart so that you can set your goals from a place of alignment with yourself.

Goals set from this place are extremely powerful, and you'll often find yourself overcoming difficult obstacles with ease. Of course, it is up to you whether you will take the time to allow your body to find its natural rhythm again. As with all of the information in this book, you have the option of experimenting with it or denying it outright. However, it is my promise to you that you will find tremendous value in the state of heart and mind coherence. It's worth a shot.

After you detox, you've got to identify what you want more than anything in the world. What experience or life situation have you been craving? It's often the ideas that we brush off as impossible that become our most motivating goals. Listen to that quiet voice within that knows what it really wants. Suspend all of your doubts and accept the big idea that you're presented with.

It will take courage to accept that your big idea is what you want out of life. Most likely it will be something that you've never even come close to achieving before, and all indicators point to the conclusion that you can't do it. In the face of this doubt you've got to accept your idea even if you don't think you can do it. This is what you want. It's not okay to deny the dream within you in order to play it safe. It may take time for you to build up the courage to pursue it and that's okay, but never allow your insignificant fears determine how you will live your life.

Now take your big idea and begin fantasising about it. Think about what it would be like if you achieved it. How would you feel if it were already your reality right this second? Find the feeling place of already enjoying this idea and then write down your goal in present-tense, emotional form. Using the present tense is very important when you write down your goal. If you use the word "will" as in, "I will do x", you are telling your subconscious mind that the idea will occur in the future. We already covered the fact that the future doesn't exist, and you'll therefore put your goal off into the future without ever making any progress towards it. You've got to tell your mind that this is what you want to experience *now*, not at some later point in time.

So for example, let's say your goal is to run a successful business that helps others get into the best shape of their life. Your goal might look like, "I am absolutely loving my life as I'm experiencing the adventure of growing my health and fitness business to new heights of success". It is filled with emotion and it's in the present tense; those are the two key components.

Setting an effective goal really is as simple as clearing your body and mind so you can get in touch with the dream that lies deep within you. If you can't find it, keep looking. It's there, I promise. Each and every one of us has an idea that we would like to achieve more than anything else. Living life causes us to create this idea, and if you want to be truly happy there is no other option but to pursue it boldly.

In summary:

1. Clear out your body by consuming no stimulants or drugs for an entire week

2. Identify what you want to experience more than anything else

3. Fantasise and feel how you would feel if you were already experiencing your goal

4. Write down your goal in present tense form

2.4.4. How to Achieve the Goals You Set

Now that you've identified what you want more than anything else and committed it to writing, it's time to lay the groundwork for the achievement of your goal.

First thing's first. You've got to cultivate a burning desire for the goal that you have chosen. If you took the time to sync your heart and mind to identify what you truly want, this step should be no problem. Basically, you want to be drooling at the mouth every single time you think about your goal. This is the kind of intensity that helps you establish the level of commitment that will be required to achieve it.

If you have a goal or dream that you just kind of want you probably won't do what it takes to achieve it. You're better off dropping all of the ideas that sound okay to you, and searching until you find that one dream that makes you say, "Now this is me!"

With a burning desire you'll be intrinsically motivated to hop out of bed early and work hard during the day. Without the burning desire, you'll need consistent motivation from sources outside of yourself, and this an unsustainable, short-sighted approach.

Next, you must accept the package deal of success. This is where the majority of us hold ourselves back from the rapid progress that is possible. The most common side effect of not accepting the package deal is procrastination and self-sabotage; if this is something that you find yourself doing, it's either because 1) you don't really want your goal, or 2) you're resisting some aspect of it.

The achievement of any goal always brings about some potential downsides. This is unavoidable and absolutely necessary for your own continued growth. You cannot delude yourself into believing that achieving your goal won't change your life and how you interact with the world around you. You've got to realise that the achievement of your goal is going to alter almost every single aspect of your life. For many of us, that is an uncomfortable idea.

Take a notebook and pen or open up a word processor and begin to brainstorm. Close your eyes and visualise your life as it would be where your goal is already your now experience. Don't fantasise, visualise. Actually get into the nitty-gritty, day to day details of your new life experience. Go through an entire day in your mind and try to predict, as realistically as you can, what your new life will be like.

- What time do you wake up in the mornings?
- What's your morning routine?
- Where do you live?
- What kind of house do you live in?
- What kind of work are you doing?

- How hard are you working?
- What's your diet like?
- Do you exercise?
- How's your family life?
- What about your social life?
- What do your finances look like?
- How do you manage your finances?
- Do you invest?
- What time do you go to sleep?
- And so on and so forth

Basically, you're bringing this future idea into your now experience by using your power of imagination. If you do this correctly you'll uncover many logical aspects of your new life that you resist. This is completely normal. These are the logical consequences of your success and you must accept them completely if you are to move forward.

Here are some more examples to get you thinking in the right directions:

Let's say your goal is to earn more money

- You might fear that you'll lose all of your money after you worked so hard to obtain it
- You might resist learning how to manage all of this money

- You might resist how differently your family and friends will treat you
- You might resist people constantly wanting something from you

Let's say your goal is to get in excellent shape:

- You might resist receiving more attention from the opposite sex
- You might resist buying new clothes and completely redoing your wardrobe
- You might resist habitually eating clean and healthy
- You might resist having to go to the gym five days a week to exercise

These are just a couple of examples, but they should give you an idea of the logical consequences that I'm talking about. Not everything about the achievement of your goal is going to be roses and rainbows. To believe so would be immature. This resistance to logical consequences is what commonly trips people up when they set goals and begin to pursue them. The more that you resist these logical consequences, the more you are going to find yourself procrastinating and otherwise holding back instead of moving forward.

Self-discipline is going to be your best friend as you move forward towards your goal. Your motivation will inevitably wax and wane like the tides of the sea, and you won't always feel like taking action. When you aren't feeling motivated, it is your self-discipline and takes the driver seat to continue moving the whole operation forward. Self-discipline, in its essence, is the ability to take action when you don't feel like doing so. It is certainly one of the more difficult character qualities to develop. The great thing, however, is that self-discipline is just like a muscle whereby you can continually train it up. You may not have the self-discipline or the talents that are required to achieve your goal at first, and this is okay. It is the growth you experience from the pursuit of your goal that makes it worthwhile in the first place.

Begin using and training your self-discipline in small and trivial ways.

- Practice holding your breath for xx seconds
- Start a new habit
- Brush your teeth with your left hand everyday
- Resist scratching an itch for at least thirty seconds
- Etc.

Basically, you want to get used to doing something that you don't feel like doing. As you practice your self-discipline will slowly develop until it reaches the level where you can set almost any goal and achieve it with ease. Self-discipline will be one of the greatest tools in your achievement toolbox. It will power through obstacles that would stop the majority of people and enable you to live the life that you really want to live.

2.4.5. Strategies for Goal Adherence

There are numerous strategies that you can use to enhance the likelihood of your success when pursuing goals. Learning these strategies will be like filling up a toolbox with different personal development tools that will come in handy at different moments in time.

Small Goals

This strategy consists of taking your one large goal and breaking it down into smaller, more manageable goals. We can easily become overwhelmed with our goal if it is something much larger than what we have ever accomplished. We magnify the goal's size in our mind and this paralyses us from taking any progressive action. The solution to this self-sabotage is to set smaller, more achievable goals that lead you in the direction of the big desire.

What sounds more doable?

1. Writing a chapter?
2. Writing and completing an entire book?

Obviously, writing a chapter sounds much more doable. And if you achieve that small goal a few times you eventually have an entire book. This whole strategy is about reducing the psychological friction we have towards 'bigness'.

How can you break your big goal down into smaller steps? Think this question through and set these more achievable goals as your priority. Before you know it you'll be enjoying your overarching desire.

Visualisation

The brain is a marvelous instrument that we've already discussed in previous chapters, and the imagination is perhaps its most valuable power. Research has recently found that your brain cannot tell the difference between an event that is vividly imagined from an event that actually takes place. Visualisation therefore, is as real as real gets to your brain. This gives you the ability to affect massively positive changes in the structure of your brain if you so wish.

Take at least thirty minutes every day to visualise yourself exactly as you'd be when your goal has already been accomplished. You must commit at least thirty minutes a day in order for this tool to really be effective. You can either visualise in one thirty minute block or split up the time into multiple sessions, the choice is yours. Just be sure to visualise for thirty minutes total, and as if it were real, not just a fantasy. Your brain is clever enough to realise when your visualisations are fantasies.

This visualisation will get you comfortable with the life you expect to live after your goal has been achieved. This instils a new confidence within you as you move boldly towards the idea you wish to bring about.

Your commitment is also renewed every time you vividly imagine your goal. It creates a pull between you and your goal so to speak. Instead of having to 'push' yourself forward, you glide effortlessly there.

Physical Reminders

Reminders are a great way to keep your goal in your mind in a way that eventually affects your habitual thinking patterns.

Take an hour or so and post your goal everywhere, and I mean everywhere—Go bananas.

- Post it on your door
- Your computer background

- Your phone background
- The dashboard of your car
- Your bathroom mirror
- Your refrigerator
- And anywhere that you'll see it often

Forget about what people might think. Seriously—who cares what they think anyway? If you have friends that make fun of you for trying to better yourself, I think it's time you start making some new friends.

Write your goal on a card as well and carry it with you everywhere you go, and read it as often as you can.

The whole purpose of this strategy is to keep your goal fresh in your mind. Every time you read it, you are impressing it farther into your subconscious mind which will automatically act upon it after enough repetition.

Mastermind Group

A mastermind group is a group of people that meet regularly to encourage and help one another achieve their individual goals. They are a great way to recharge your batteries and receive valuable insight on your current challenges.

You'll have a group of people supporting you and holding you accountable for forward progress towards your goal. They'll often believe in you more than you believe in yourself, and this is extremely helpful in getting through the inevitable lows of goal pursuit. They'll pick you up when you're down and keep your spirits high as you march on towards eventual success.

Finding a mastermind group will be something that you'll have to put effort into. Usually, you'll have to create one yourself. You must find like-minded individuals and set up weekly meetings, either online using a tool like Skype or in person, that everyone can attend. You can find these individuals in forums, meet-ups, or other events where they might congregate. Get creative.

Enjoy the Journey!

You're much more likely to succeed if you thoroughly enjoy the path to success. In fact, it can be said that the journey is the whole point! You don't go on a vacation just so you can get to the end of it, and likewise, you wouldn't climb a mountain just to stand at the peak. You do all of these things because the process of getting there itself is enjoyable.

It's the exact same thing with your goal. Learn to enjoy the process of learning and growing that you're experiencing. You know what you've set out to achieve, and you know that you'll reach it as long as you keep moving forward day after day.

There's no need to rush. Slow down and take the time to enjoy the view, but keep yourself moving forwards. Once you've got some momentum, do everything within your power to maintain it; an object in motion tends to stay in motion, and an object at rest tends to stay at rest. But always, always remember that the purpose of your goal is to improve your life in the here and now.

2.5

CHAPTER 7:
HABITS

2.5.1. Introduction

Up to this point, we've been focusing on high level ideas that are critical to a successful life. As we move into this chapter, we'll be bringing these higher level ideas into concrete action; this is where the rubber meets the road.

We pay much too little attention to our habits, and our results suffer because of this. Proper care and attention must be given to both our habitual behaviours and our habitual ways of thinking. Without becoming aware of our habits, we will tend to run on autopilot and we'll have major difficulty creating the life that we want.

Habits are one of the fundamental principles of personal development. In this chapter I will present to you valuable information for a proper understanding of both the importance of habits and how to go about changing them.

As the great Jim Rohn said, "In order to have more, you must first become more."

Let's dive in!

2.5.2. Your Habits Make Your Life

Your habits are one of the first areas in your life that you need to take a look at. The success in every area of your life largely depends upon your habits. Aristotle said it best when he said, "You are what you repeatedly do . . ."

Our habits make or break us for better or worse, and quite often, we allow our habits to run on autopilot without ever realising that we can do differently. We mistakenly assume that we must continue to do a thing a certain way because that's how we've always done it in the past. We think that we are not morning people because we've always woken up late, or we think that we are just lazy because we've never worked super hard. These are just two examples of how habits can quickly turn into self-concepts of who we think we are.

Everything you will ever have or do in your life (achievement wise) will most certainly be a result of your habits. Your habits are how you spend your time, and how you spend your time equals your results. If you have the habit of waking up late and lounging around for most of the day, what results do you realistically expect?

Very often we delude ourselves into thinking that we're on track for the goals that we have set. We feel like we're making progress and that success is inevitable. But, if we take a closer look at how we're spending the majority of our time, we'll often find a very different picture.

The easiest thing to do in the world is to pretend that our habits are supporting our goals, because it's one of the hardest things in the world to change a habit. The beautiful thing to realise however, is that habits can be changed! We can change who we are by how we habitually spend our time, and new results can be ours!

The Compound Effect

Darren Hardy wrote an absolutely phenomenal book on the power of habits. His primary message was that small actions repeated consistently add up to *huge* results over time.

Whenever you take a short-term look at your habits, it's easy to blow them off because they don't look like they make that much of a difference. How big a deal is it to sleep for an extra hour a night? It doesn't seem like much from a daily perspective, but let's step back and look at it from a larger perspective. If you sleep one extra hour a night, you're sleeping for an extra nine full forty hour working weeks per year! Do you realise what you could do with over two months extra working time? Let's step back even farther now and look at it from a five year perspective. At just one seemingly insignificant hour a night, you're now sleeping over forty full forty hour working weeks; that's ten and a half months of time wasted! But, let's step back even farther to a ten year perspective. At just one extra hour a night you're now wasting almost **two years** of full working time by that seemingly insignificant hour. I think you get the point. Small things done repeatedly add up.

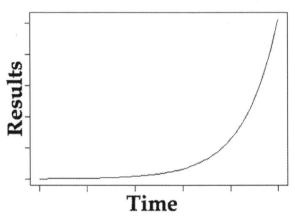

THE COMPOUND EFFECT

You can think of the compound effect as an exponential curve. During the first period of time nothing seems to happen. Your results stay pretty close to exactly where they were and you can't really tell a difference. However, if you persist in the repetition of the habit, eventually the graph tilts in your favor and your results begin to accumulate fast! The toughest part is getting past that initial time period where you aren't seeing any results from your efforts.

The amount of time that is required for your results to begin dramatically changing will be different for each habit. For some habits, such as rising early, you will quickly see the fruits of your labor as your results compound quickly. However, for others, such as daily meditation, it will take much longer for your results to begin to compound.

You can also think of the compound effect as planting an apple tree. The results that you desire can be thought of as the apples of this tree. It would be insane to think that you could plant the tree and in one month collect the apples wouldn't it? In fact, if you started with just the tree seed, it would be insane to think that you would even *see* the tree let alone the fruits for a long while. The same thing is true of your habits. You've got to plant the seed, allow the roots to grow deep, and eventually your little tree will sprout through the ground. Continue to nurture it through watering (desire) and sunshine (persistence), and before you know it you'll be sitting beneath its shade biting into the sweet apples of your efforts.

The biggest tripping point for most people is expecting results immediately after beginning a new habit. Society has conditioned us to expect results *now*, and if we don't see them within a short while we quickly get impatient and drop the habit. It's time for us to slow down and mature our perspective habit development.

The game of personal development is a game of long ball. It's a marathon not a sprint. By setting realistic expectations you allow yourself to persist when your seed is still growing. You know that if you continue to water and nurture the seed eventually you will have your fruits.

The Snowball Effect

This effect is similar to the compound effect, but it addresses a different aspect of habits. This Snowball Effect states that whenever you change just one habit, that positive change snowballs into bigger and bigger changes.

This effect played out significantly in my own path of personal development. I began with installing the single habit of making my bed every morning after I woke up. That's it. Nothing more than that little five minute action. That would seem insignificant wouldn't it? That small change then progressed into the habit of keeping my personal areas very clean, neat, and organised. That change then led to the adoption of a one hour a day meditation practice which then led to the habits of personal productivity. And on and on this snowball rolled until my life had been completely reworked from the ground up.

It's not necessarily that the small habit change is the cause of the other changes. It seems to be the other way around, wherein the single **decision** to change puts the snowball in motion. Without the firm *decision*, the snowball effect could not take place. Regardless of whether you change some major habit or even a tiny one like making your bed, the decision to change sets in motion the process of life change.

Goal Achievement through Habits

In order to achieve a goal you must cultivate the habits that will lead to its attainment.

The first and foremost cause of the achievement of *any* goal is the *decision* to achieve it. After this decision has been made, the next step is to begin altering your habits until you are constantly on the correct path.

Your collective habits can be thought of like the foundation of a great building. In order to build anything you've got to first have a foundation upon which to build. Your habits are this structurally sound beginning point on top of which you will build your incredible building of success. Just remember, your building of success can't be built very high without the proper foundation.

It's tough to take a look at your current habits and admit to yourself that some of them aren't supporting you. It may make you feel like a failure. I know it did for me. It made me feel like I wasn't perfect after all, and that I did have a lot of work to do on myself. As young adults, we often fall into the trap of thinking that we're already perfect and that success is inevitable. The quicker we can mature and realise that success is inevitable only if the right causes are present, the better. Then we can release the idea of ourselves as a flawless being and really get to work.

Self-acceptance is a crucial component of the life change process. Regardless of where you may be standing, you are still worthy of love, happiness, and success. Your worthiness can never be taken away from you by anyone but yourself. It you can look at your current situation, your habits, your goals, and fully accept that you want to change, your journey is well under way. Again I want to emphasise the point that the *decision* to be successful, and the willingness to do whatever it takes, is the first step to your eventual success.

Honest self assessment is one of the essential tools of a well-equipped personal development tool box. It's easy for us to construct mental ideas of ourselves that don't resemble reality. Do your best to take an objective look at your thoughts, your habits, your decisions, and your life in order to see where you can do better. If you don't know what needs improving, how can you improve?

This type of honesty will quickly reveal that you do have flaws and that there will always be ways in which you can improve. Do not allow this realisation to have any effect whatsoever on your self-esteem. To expect perfection from yourself is to expect the impossible. The beauty of the human species, and the larger Universe in general, is the quirks that make each of us so incredibly unique. You aren't perfect, and you never will be. Stop holding yourself to standards of impossibility. Accept who you are and love yourself unconditionally, because no one is more worthy of your love than you.

2.5.3. Identifying Supportive Habits

Now that we've covered the importance of honest self-assessment, it's time to begin identifying what habits would help accelerate you towards your goal. There are a number of ways to do this and I'll share with you the two that I think are the most valuable.

Visualisation

Visualisation is a powerful way to determine which habits will assist you in achieving what you set out to achieve. Begin to build a picture in your mind of how you want your life to be, and the kind of person that you want to be. There are no right or wrong answers here. Step into the shoes of your childhood self and allow your mind to dream without any limitations.

It's best to reverse engineer your mental picture. Start with your goal in mind and visualise it as if it were real, as if you had already achieved it. Now go a step farther and visualise your life/lifestyle now that your goal has been achieved.

- Where do you live?
- What do you spend your time doing?
- What time do you wake up?
- What kinds of food do you eat?
- What are your exercise habits?
- Who are your friends?
- Do you have a family?
- What are your favourite activities?

Once you've visualised both your dream being achieved and your lifestyle as a result of that, dig even deeper and see the you that is living this life. This part is critical. Visualise deep enough that instead of merely fantasising, you actually see the person you need to become.

This, again, is a huge sticking point for most practitioners of visualisation. They don't visualise in enough depth, and so they never see the contrast between their current life experience and what it is they desire. Visualisation is most useful in building a clear picture of the type of person you must become in order to achieve your goal. Your success will be a result of you building a clear mental picture of who you want to be, and then stepping towards that picture every day.

When you imagine what your goal will require you to become, there's a chance that you may not like it. You may resist moulding yourself into that person because of how difficult it is going to be. If you resist your goal in this way, you will fall victim to procrastination and other forms of self-sabotage. Figure out the price you must pay, and then determine to pay that price no matter what.

When you practice realistic visualisation, you'll find a number of habits that I like to call overarching habits. These are habits that will support you in any pursuit in life as they pertain to general well-being. These include:

- Waking up early
- Being productive
- Daily exercise
- Healthy eating
- Positive thinking
- Belief in oneself
- Daily meditation or calmness practice
- Decisiveness
- Continual learning

These are all habits that will move you forward in any area of your life.

Your task is to start implementing these different practices into your life one by one. Eventually, each of these practices will be put on autopilot, meaning you won't have to think about them; they'll run on their own.

Interviews/Mentors

Seek out the top performers in your particular interests and get to know them. The more time you spend with people who are successful in life, the clearer you'll see where you still need to develop. You'll begin to see why some are successful and why others aren't, and how you can place yourself in the first group. You'll find certain habits that the top performers have taken the time to cultivate, and you'll begin to install them in your own life.

The value of a personal mentor cannot be overstated. To have someone in your life that already is where you want to be can be tremendously helpful. You'll have access to their wisdom, and the ability to learn from their mistakes. There is no better strategy that will accelerate you along your path. Instead of reinventing the wheel, you'll be learning directly from someone who already knows how to create it. This saves you time and tremendous frustration.

Use the internet to seek out the people that are doing what you want to do, and then figure out how you can be of service to them. Nobody wants to help a moocher.

There is an easy way to gain access to top performers if you're having trouble finding one in person. Consume the material they produce. If you constantly fill your mind with the thoughts and ideas of the top performers, then by osmosis you'll begin to think that way yourself. This doesn't mean that all you have to do is listen to the audio tapes, read the books, and you'll be successful. I made this mistake for a number of years. I thought that if I just read the books, then everything would happen in my life; not true. The benefit of the books and programs is to assist you in your own pursuits. You then need to put what you have learnt into action. Don't mistake them for the end itself, they're simply a means to the end.

2.5.4. How to Install New Habits

Your habits can be thought of as programs that are installed on your hard drive (your brain). Habits are memorised patterns of doing things in a certain way. This is what allows our brains to be so efficient. Think about how slowly life would move if you had to think about how to tie your shoe every single morning. Habit is what puts behaviour on autopilot so your thinking mind has more computing power to work on the current challenges you're facing. Our habits are rooted in the subconscious mind, and therefore, won't be apparent to us unless we *deliberately* look for them.

Habits almost seem as if they're happening *to* us in a strange sort of way. A huge tripping point for many is mistakenly assuming that they are *choosing* to do what they do. Very little, if any, of our daily activities are chosen before we do them. The ego's biggest badge of honour is that it thinks it chooses what to do and when to do it.

Instead of viewing ourselves in accordance with our habits (e.g. I'm lazy because I don't work out), we can understand that the habit is a learned behaviour, and therefore, has nothing to do with our character. Be careful not to develop a negative self-image just because of some faulty programming work. We can literally be anybody we want to be, and this is because the power of the brain.

We can identify new habits that we want to install on our hardware, and then do what's necessary to install them. If you base your self-concept on your current habits, you are a prisoner to your programming and lack the ability to change. You must begin to release your sense of identity from who you currently are, and realise that you are something far greater than your thoughts, your personality, or your habits. With this realisation comes the ability to alter these at will.

The Strategy

Steve Pavlina wrote an excellent article on strategic habit change that I want to share with you and elaborate on. I have used it with tremendous success in my own life, as it's a phenomenal way to go about altering our learned behaviours.

The majority of failed attempts to change habits occur because we underestimate the power of the subconscious mind. We blindly rush in and think that we can change a habit overnight without any planning or strategy involved. This is a recipe for failure.

Approach habit change as if you're going to war. You can't go straight after the enemy without planning and expect to realistically win. A fixed habit is an adversary worthy of the most strategic planning.

A proper strategy for successful habit change can be thought of in three stages; the beginning game, the middle game, and the end game. Let's explore each of these in detail.

The beginning game

This is the stage of preparation where you collect as much information as possible. You're going to learn everything you possibly can about the new habit that you wish to install, and you're also going to learn everything about the habit that you no longer want.

For example, if the habit you want to install is to eat healthy, you would consume everything you could get your hands on pertaining to proper nutrition. You would talk to people who do eat healthy, and identify the mindset that they have towards eating. You would read books, watch videos, and do anything you can to learn more about nutrition. You would also look within to learn why you currently eat unhealthy. Both the outside and inside components are essential.

This learning allows you to get an accurate view of the habit that you desire to install.

The middle game

This is the stage where you develop a plan of action. Your primary focus is to strategically determine how you can successfully make the habit change. This usually means setting up systems to support you during the habit change process.

Going back to the example of eating healthy; your strategy might be to clean out all of the junk food in your house, precook your meals a week in advance, join a group of people that will hold you accountable, post pictures of your ideal body around your environment, sign up for personal training, etc.

Your aim is to increase the odds of your success by as much as possible. If you executed well at the beginning stage you should have an easy time developing a strategy. Use everything you learned and figure out how to put in action.

The end game

This is where the rubber meets the road and you actually begin changing your behaviour. If you attempt to change your behavior before you have acquired the knowledge and developed a sound plan, your chances of success are slim to none.

The most effective way to execute your strategy is to perform a thirty day trial. A thirty day trial is an experiment where you will execute your desired behaviour every single day, without fail, for thirty days in a row.

After this initial thirty days, the new habit will be on autopilot and you can relax a tiny bit. These thirty days are typically enough to push the new behaviour down into your subconscious mind. However, the most important thing is that you perform your new habit every day for the full thirty days! If you slip up even one day, you've got to start over for another thirty. Until the new habit is firmly rooted in your subconscious, one missed day is sufficient to set you back an entire week or two.

Self-Discipline

It's no surprise that self-discipline is required to change habits, and in fact required to live a successful life. If you cannot control yourself, you cannot control your life situation. This is a simple truth of life. Look at any top performer and you will find high levels of self-discipline every single time. Success isn't possible without it.

The great thing is that self-discipline can be developed and trained very much like a muscle as we discussed earlier. By going through the process of habit change, not only are you installing new beneficial habits that will pay off, but you're also developing your self-discipline.

As you tackle one habit after the other, they become easier to replace. Just like anything in life, the more you do it the better you get at it. Once your self-discipline reaches a certain level, changing habits will become ridiculously easy. You'll then be in the very pleasurable position of being able to fashion your life in any way you choose.

However, developing your self-discipline to this level isn't easy and it takes a long time. But this doesn't matter. Ten years from now would you rather have the high level of self-discipline required for achievement? Or would you rather take it easy for those ten years and be in the same place you currently are?

Habit change is a game of long ball. You've got to start thinking long term in order to strategically place yourself in a position in which you have the greatest chances for success. This means installing habits that will assist you in achieving your dreams.

Give up the desire for instant gratification to develop a longer perspective. It's easy to eat, sleep, and have sex, but not so easy to wake up early, manage your time well, and meditate daily. The lower level instant gratification activities are natural and we'll gravitate towards them by default. A conscious effort is required to overcome these lower desires and develop a life that will truly fulfil you. Control your base impulses so you may develop into the successful being that you know you can be.

2.6

CHAPTER 8:
THE LAW OF ATTRACTION

2.6.1. Introduction

Many people have a very deluded idea of what exactly the Law of Attraction (LOA) is these days. Due to mass popularisation of the law, it has been made to seem like a very simple, almost magical process in which you just imagine what you want and *"BAM!"* it's there. Not so.

This magnificent law of the Universe is more complex than what it has been marketed to be. The disappointing thing is that these false expectations have caused many people to discount the Law of Attraction as something that doesn't work, and only because it didn't produce the desired results.

This law *always* works. It literally cannot fail. It is how the Universe has and will operate for eternity. This great law is very similar to the law of gravity; you can't see it and you often aren't consciously aware of it. However, if you observe closely you can very easily see the law in action.

Learning how to consciously use the Law of Attraction to enhance your life is a process that takes time. Not only is it a skill that must be cultivated, but the actual manifestations will take time to come about as well. Patience is one of those key qualities of living a successful life.

It is my intention to explain this law in a way that is both easy to understand, yet comprehensive in its coverage. I want you to understand the working basis of the law and how you can put it to use in your life.

I don't ask you to believe me whatsoever. To accept anything on blind faith is the surest way to following the crowd. I ask you to take these ideas and think deeply about them, and then suspend your doubts and put this knowledge to the test in your life. How can you ever know whether something works or doesn't work without giving it a serious try? Prematurely assuming the Law of Attraction doesn't work could be one of the biggest mistakes on your path of growth.

Let's say that you're on the fence about testing it out; really, what's the worst that could happen? You try it for thirty days and nothing happens, okay cool, now you know from your own experience. Now, what's the best thing that could happen? You could unlock vast amounts of previously "impossible" opportunities as you begin creating your life consciously. Sounds like an obvious choice to me.

As with all things in life, the worthwhile results are only achieved through consistent effort. I urge you to seriously consider these ideas and perform more research if you're interested. These ideas do have the power to change your life for the better.

2.6.2. Everything is Vibration

The most fundamental law of the Universe, by which the LOA operates, is the Law of Vibration.

Every single thing from the largest stars and planets in space, all the way down to the tiniest grain of sand, is in a constant state of vibration.

This can be difficult to believe as everything around us seems so solid. If everything is vibration why can't I put my hand right through this computer that I'm now typing on? The answer is found within the terms frequency and arrangement.

Your brain is a marvellous instrument which we talked quite a bit about in the earlier chapters. It is so marvellous that it has taken the vibrations all around you, and learned how to translate it into your "reality" in a way so that you can't even recognise its vibration. Think about it . . . What are the colours that you perceive? If you've studied any science then you know that colour is just a vibration at a particular frequency. What are the sounds that you hear? They are nothing more but vibrations that your brain has translated in order to make sense out of it.

This magnificent translation of vibration happens with every single one of your five physical sense; tasting, touching, smelling, seeing, and hearing. It's all translation of different frequencies of vibration!

From this knowledge, it can be stated that your entire "reality" is all within your head. There is nothing "out there" even though it seems like it. If you are perceiving something that seems to be outside of yourself, you are actually making these perceptions inside your own head. It's the case of the popular question, "if a tree falls in a forest and nobody's there to hear it, does it make a sound?" The idea is that you cannot experience your reality without *actively* perceiving it and this is the fundamental basis of the Law of Attraction.

Even after you have proof that everything around you is vibration it is still very hard for us to grasp this on an emotional level (this just emphasises how weak our logic is compared to our emotions). Logically accepting this truth is much different than actually believing this truth and *applying* it to your life.

In order to begin consciously creating your reality, begin believing that everything is vibration. Take some time out of your day, and sit and just attempt to visualise the vibrational nature of everything around you. Quiet your mind and really *feel* the vibration of the sounds and the air around you. Suspend any doubts you may have for just a few minutes and give it a go. I think you'll be pleasantly surprised.

When you begin experimenting with vibration and the Law of Attraction, it's very common that your sense of reality will be ungrounded for a few weeks. Your world may be turned upside down as you are shifting your beliefs about the very nature of reality. It is naturally uncomfortable to let go of what you know and start exploring the unknown. Even if you can predict a greener pasture on the other side of the exploration, it doesn't change the uncomfortable nature of it.

I tell you this so that you are prepared emotionally to begin experimenting with consciously creating your life. We have been raised to believe that we hold no power over our lives, that we are victims to circumstances and events, but this is not true. We innately possess the power to create our lives, and this is done through cooperation with the Law of Attraction.

Like Attracts Like

The fundamental principle of the Law of Vibration is that vibrations of similar frequency are drawn together.

Think about two droplets of water that are slowly moving towards each other. What happens as they get closer? They eventually get close enough that they attract each other and become one droplet of water instead of two separate ones. This occurs because they are of like vibration. Now, think about the same phenomena with a droplet of water and a droplet of oil. No matter how close you put them together they will not become one with each other. This is because their vibrations are too different from one another.

This is the idea that the Law of Attraction is based on. If you want to bring about something in your life, regardless of what it is, begin vibrating at a level that is congruent with your desired reality (we'll discuss how to do this in more detail later on).

This is such a huge idea! Think about it! If 1). Everything is vibration and, 2). Vibrations of similar frequencies are drawn together and, 3). You have the ability to control your vibration; then you can most certainly control the conditions of your life!

The problem comes about whenever we attempt to control our reality without first adjusting our vibration. No amount of physical manipulation will create the world that we wish to see. All of the work is done on the inside, in our minds. This means that no amount of action alone will produce the results that we desire. However, once we gain the ability to condition our minds to our desired frequencies of vibration, our physical reality quickly follows suit and reflects back to us our new vibration.

Take the time to think deeply about these ideas and see if they don't make sense to you both logically and emotionally. If you think long and hard enough you will come to the same conclusions that the great leaders of humanity's past have all come to: that is, **we create our own reality**.

2.6.3. Claim Your Power

In order to begin creating a life that you want there is one necessary requirement to accept. You must accept complete and total, one hundred percent responsibility for your life experience.

This is a very common sticking point to the average individual. Think about it, is it easier to blame everything around you for your misfortunes? Or is it easier to accept that life is the way you have chosen to create it? Of course it's easier to place blame anywhere other than yourself.

Creation is impossible until this idea of complete responsibility is totally embraced. If you don't think that you're responsible for your life experience, how could you possibly create something different? I understand that it's tough, but it's a requirement.

Here's a list of where a lot of us place the responsibility for our lives. Check yourself by it and see if you've been placing others in charge of your life:

- The government
- Your parents
- Your employer
- Your school
- The 'hand you were dealt'
- Your genes
- Your ancestors

Whenever you blame something outside of yourself for the way your life currently is, you are giving your power away. You convince yourself that you have no power, and that there's nothing you can do because you aren't in control.

This false idea could not be further from the truth. The truth is that you are an extremely powerful being with vast reservoirs of potential untapped within you. Deep down you know this, but you also recognise that developing this vast potential won't be the easy path in life. You know that giving your power away, and playing the victim role, is the easier path. You recognise that accepting responsibility for your life is a big step from where you currently are.

Perhaps it's the opposite though. Perhaps life is much harder when you deny who you really are, when you deny your true power, instead of rising up and taking control of your life.

You may have had a tough and unfair life up to this point but understand that that is quite irrelevant. It doesn't matter what's happened in the past, and it's pointless to use that as an excuse for why you're dissatisfied with your life today. Accept that your life was the way it was, and now is the way it is, and if anything is to change it is completely up to you.

Developing the Power of Your Thoughts

You now understand the incredible power that your thoughts have, and now it's time to understand that you do have the ability to completely control them.

Napoleon Hill once said something that I really enjoyed. He stated that your mind is the only thing which you have complete and unquestionable control over, and that this is a fact so astounding that it seems to place the mind of man into close relationship with Infinite Intelligence.

Be careful not to make the mistake of assuming that just because you do have the ability to completely control your thoughts, that you have been exercising this power. We can very easily go an entire week without being aware of one single thought. This autopilot thinking is how you create a life by default, and that usually means a life of the status quo.

Gaining control over your thoughts is the fundamental skill to consciously create your life. It can be developed, but only with consistent, dedicated practice. The idea of watching every single thought you think may be an overwhelming idea initially, and that's how it's supposed to be. However, as you practice, the task becomes easier and easier. Begin to choose your thoughts consciously until you make the positive mental attitude that you desire a habit. Once this is accomplished, you won't have to be as aware of your thoughts as they will only require a 'tune up' here and there to get back on track.

Your emotions can also help to ease the overwhelm of watching every single thought. Instead of being aware of your thoughts, you can place your awareness on your emotions which tend to be easier to notice. Whenever you feel good, you know that your thoughts have been good; and whenever you feel magnificent, you know that your thoughts have been magnificent. Whenever you feel terrible, you know that your thoughts have been terrible; and so on. You are always creating in accordance with your thoughts, which are in direct relation to your emotions.

Whenever you notice yourself thinking negatively or feeling bad, give your full efforts to transforming that negativity into positivity. The first few weeks you attempt to do this will be quite difficult, but practice makes perfect. Eventually, you'll get to a point of such thought control that you won't tolerate negative emotion for even a second.

Your point of power is always in the present moment. You cannot create in the past or the future; only right now. Even when you're remembering your past or imagining your future, you're always doing so in the present moment.

What you *choose* to focus on in each moment of your life will be exactly what your life resembles.

How You Give Your Power Away

Throughout the early years of our lives, we've been taught to give our power away. We have been taught that events and circumstances outside of us have power over our lives. We were taught that it is completely natural to react to whatever is happening around us. We were taught that you cannot control your responses to the world.

All of these ideas are incredibly limiting.

The fact is, we are all in complete control of our lives regardless of our circumstances. Anytime you allow something outside of yourself to affect your mood or thoughts, you are giving your power away.

Let's look at a few examples:

- You're driving in your car, and the driver in the lane next to you suddenly swerves into your lane and cuts you off. This makes you feel angry and frustrated

- You're at a restaurant and you receive very poor service from the wait staff. This irritates you and ruins your evening

- You're having lunch with a friend and this friend only talks about the bad things happening in her life. This makes you feel depressed and down yourself

- You expect a concert to be a certain way but it doesn't quite pan out the way you had hoped. You feel disappointed because your expectations weren't met

In all of these examples, you placed your inner emotional state at the mercy of uncontrollable situations. It's apparent that you don't have any direct control over what happens around you, but **you do have control over your response to what happens around you**.

The vast majority of the world will only *react* their entire lives. They are like pinballs being bounced from bumper to bumper as the happenings of their life control who they are. This is animal-like behaviour and not worthy of who we are. Instead, as conscious human beings we have "response-ability", or **the ability to choose our response**! This may seem like a burden but it is a true gift.

Imagine what it would be like to always feel calm, collected, and happy, regardless of what's going on in your life. Deep in debt and almost bankrupt? No problem, you have the ability to choose your response to that. You can react to that and feel really bad about your situation, become depressed, go into denial and increase your debt as a result or you can choose your response and view it as an interesting challenge.

This reveals that there really are no "problems" in our reality, but only problems inside our own minds. We think of problems and difficulty and sure enough, that's exactly what the Universe delivers. That is the Law of Attraction at work.

Begin to become aware of how much psychic energy you use to *create* needless worry and anxiety. We spend so much time thinking of what people think about us, what might go wrong, how we're messing up, and so many other pointless things. This drains us both physically and emotionally, and dramatically reduces our quality of life. Release your need for control. Let what happens happen, and resolve to be happy no matter what. Your happiness is a choice.

Now you may be saying at this point that you only think about problems because that's all you experience. This is a valid point, but only until you fully recognise your power as a conscious human being.

Let's look at an example:

Bryan is a hardworking, honest guy that finds his life filled with hardship after hardship. One week he loses his job, and then his car breaks down and he doesn't have the money to fix it. The next week, his laptop is stolen from his workspace as he goes to use the restroom. On and on it goes for Bryan.

*These things are happening to Bryan because he is emitting a vibration (through his thoughts) that is in harmony with the vibration of hardship. Now Bryan might argue that the only reason he thinks thoughts of hardship is because that is all he has ever experienced. However, Bryan does possess the ability to direct his mind to think about **whatever he chooses**. If he would begin right this second to eliminate thoughts of hardship from his mind, these problems would slowly disappear from his life. They wouldn't all disappear at once, but little by little as he shifted his habitual thinking patterns.*

It all comes down to your innately powerful ability as a creator to direct your mind. This is the most powerful ability of all of us, and yet it is so underutilised! How many people do you know that experience the same situation over and over again? They end up in the same type of relationships even though they don't want them. It seems odd that they would do such crazy things, but it is because they haven't yet exercised their power to change their minds.

Increase Your Awareness

If you wish to begin creating a life of your choosing then it's necessary that you increase your awareness of how you're currently thinking.

You can accomplish this in a variety of ways, but the most effective that I've found is meditation. By quieting the mind and becoming aware of what's going on inside your mind for just ten or fifteen minutes a day, you increase your awareness throughout your day. The more you increase your awareness, the more you grow. Meditation is the act of sitting quietly and observing your thoughts without getting involved.

You can also carry a small notebook with you wherever you go, and use it as a tool for raising your awareness. Anytime you notice that you're feeling bad, stop whatever you're doing, and open up your notebook. Explore the feeling of negativity and trace it back to its cause. At the root of every negative feeling you'll find that it is nothing other than a situation where you have given your power away. Every negative emotion occurs as a result of you allowing something outside of your control to direct your inner state.

By using both of these practices you will begin to see just how often you give your power away. Even with practice you'll still give your power away at times, but you'll certainly get better over time. As you increase your ability to choose a response, you increase your ability to create a life of your choosing. So we find that the effort to gain control over your responses to life is the most worthwhile effort you could ever offer.

2.6.4. Your Thoughts Create Your Reality

Now that we understand everything in the entire Universe is vibration at its most fundamental level, we begin to understand just how the law of attraction works.

There are three planes of existence that we exist in simultaneously. These are the spiritual plane, the mental plane, and the physical plane in descending order of frequency of vibration.

The three planes can be represented in this manner:

Spiritual—> Mental—> Physical

The spiritual plane is the highest frequency of vibration and the building block for everything mental and physical; the mental plane is the second highest frequency of vibration; and the physical plane is the lowest frequency of vibration. The higher the frequency of a vibration, the more potent it is and the less perceivable it is to our five senses.

For example, the chair that you are sitting in is vibrating at a relatively low frequency. So you have the ability to see it, touch it, taste it, and otherwise sense it with the physical senses. However, your thoughts are vibrating at a much higher frequency, and so you cannot sense them with any sense other than your hearing.

The odd thing is, we focus the majority of our attention on the physical plane which has the lowest potential to affect our lives. Instead of focusing our attention on the mental plane where our efforts can reveal incredible results, we are content to bang around on the physical plane.

From this model of reality we can see that action is one of the least powerful vibrations. Now don't get me wrong, action is absolutely essential to experiencing success of any level, but the action is really secondary to what is going on inside the mind.

All of us must begin to become more aware of what exactly we're doing with the incredible power of our minds. We place our faith in the visible while completely ignoring the more powerful invisible components of the Universe. This is easily seen in the old saying, "I'll believe it when I see it". This statement is the epitome of faith in the physical with an ignorance of everything else.

I understand that it's not easy to believe the idea that we create our own realities through the power of thought. We have been raised to believe that everything happens by chance and that we are victims of this unpredictable Universe. We were taught that the physical is what matters, and thought and spirit are nothing but an afterthought or perhaps a useless exploration.

The tricky thing is, if you don't believe that your thoughts create your reality, then you end up creating a reality in which you don't have the ability to create your reality . . . Get it? So even if you don't believe that you have the power to do so, you always have and always will create your life experience through your thoughts. The only way to truly discover this for yourself is to set your old beliefs aside, and jump into this idea head first.

I want you to get an idea of this vibration thing so we're going to do a little experiment.

1. Go to a place that is as least physically stimulating as possible (quiet, dark, room temperature, neutral smell, etc.)

2. Lie down on the floor with your arms at your side and take ten deep breaths. Inhale through your nose all the way down to the bottom of your stomach, and then exhale through your mouth being sure to push out every last bit of air

3. As you finish your deep breathing begin to focus your full attention on the rise and fall of your chest and belly as you breathe normally (do this for about five minutes until your mind calms down)

4. Now tune in and just attempt to feel the vibration of your body. Turn your attention to a particular body part, such as your foot, and see if you can feel its vibration

5. Continue to feel for the vibration until you find it. It's there

If you give this experiment a sincere effort, you should have literally felt how your body is nothing but vibration. It is a very subtle feeling but there is most certainly a high rate of vibration. If you can't feel it then don't worry. Try it a few times if you'd like, and you should be able to get it then.

This is an incredible experiment because we can actually experience the vibration instead of thinking about it. Now here's the really cool part:

Try this experiment again in the exact same manner but this time, after you find the vibration, think thoughts of happiness, love, puppies, or whatever feels really good to you. Then turn your attention to the vibration once again and you should be able to discern a difference. Now, turn your thoughts towards hatred, revenge, and jealousy, and once again become aware of your vibration. Again, you should be able to tell a difference.

What this shows us is that thoughts of positivity vibrate at a higher frequency than thoughts of negativity. You can literally feel the difference in your body when you think differently.

Now we know that we can literally control our vibration by **choosing** to entertain different thoughts in our minds. Since vibrations of like frequency are drawn together, it is therefore clearly evident that by thinking thoughts of a positive nature, we attract more positive into our lives by altering our own vibration. This gives us the complete power to control our life experience, not through direct physical action, but by taking the time to consistently raise our vibrational frequency.

CARLA SCHESSER

The brain can be likened to a broadcasting station which is constantly emitting the vibrations of your thoughts. Every single thought that you think is translated into vibration and then sent out into the Universe. The Universe receives your message and then delivers to you the experiences and circumstances that are the exact same vibrational frequency as that message.

From some of the latest discoveries in science we know that thoughts are literally "things" and they have an impact on the world around us. We only mistake them as "not real" because we can't sense them with any of the regular physical senses.

I present all of this to begin to unravel the mystery of why things happen in your life the way that they do. Nothing happens by chance or by "luck". The Universe operates by exact law. Our objective in living a successful life is to learn these unfailing laws and adjust ourselves into accordance with them.

What are Emotions?

The emotions you feel on a moment to moment basis are a shortcut to recognising how you're vibrating. Your body is extremely intelligent, and it has its own way of interpreting and decoding vibration so that you can be more aware of how you are creating your experience.

Whenever you feel good, you are vibrating at a high frequency and whenever you feel bad, you are vibrating at a low frequency. There are many different frequencies of vibration, and this is the cause for the variety of different emotions that you can experience. However, for simplicity's sake, it is easier to think in terms of either good feeling/high vibration or bad feeling/low vibration.

Your emotions remove the burden of watching every thought. Without them, if you wanted to consciously create your own reality you would have to watch every single thought that emitted from your brain. This would be a huge task and almost impossible to do in the real world. Your body shortcuts this task by feeling emotion which more easily lets you know where you're vibrating.

The emotional system is so incredibly simple and it works one hundred percent of the time.

Begin to become more aware of how you're feeling on a moment to moment basis. Once you are aware, you then have the ability to alter your vibration which then alters your emotions. This is essentially the process of reality creation.

2.6.5. Decisions, Decisions

Another law of the Universe is the law of Cause and Effect. This law states that for every reaction there is an equal and opposite reaction.

The cause and effect mindset is very ingrained in us, and this is a wonderful thing. However, the problem is that we mistake what a real cause is.

We commonly look at success and we can easily see that it is an effect, no arguments there. The mix up comes when we attempt to discern the cause of someone's success. Whenever we attempt to discern the cause of success the most common place to look is towards action, or even the thinking of the individual. We say that he or she took this and this action while thinking these and these thoughts, and this made her successful. Seems logical right? But in fact, these actions and thoughts are an effect themselves.

The real cause of success is a **decision** to be successful. Another word for decision is **intention**.

At some point, every single successful person decided that they would be successful. After that decision was made, the proper thoughts and actions eventually followed. This decision occurs in one single moment, but it's usually preceded by much contemplation or even an unsettling event. The key takeaway here is that the entire future of your life can change with one clear, committed decision.

Ralph Waldo Emerson once said, "Once you make a decision, the universe conspires to make it happen" and once you begin to consciously make clear choices, you'll very quickly see the truth in this statement. It's as if the Universe is sitting here waiting to give us whatever we want if we'll only ask clearly, loudly, and for one thing at a time. As soon as you make a clear decision the Universe rushes to your aid, and mysteriously brings you everything you need to know, do, all the people you need to meet, and anything else required to make that decision a reality.

So many of us never fully develop our decision making skills, and this is a shame. We're not taught how to make decisions in school, and we then go through life without the knowledge of how to change our lives for the better.

If there's something that you really want in life, stop wasting time wondering if it's something that you can achieve. Stop going around and telling your idea to people and asking for their feedback. Stop caring if your idea is even ""realistic", just make a clear, committed decision to make it so, and if you stick to that decision, it must become so.

Was Bill Gates' dream of putting a computer in every home "realistic"? Was the Wright Brothers' dream to build a flying machine "realistic"? How about Henry

Ford's dream to mass produce the automobile, was that "realistic"? Of course not. If you were around these guys whenever all they had were their dreams, you would have probably told them to grow up and get a job. Fortunately for us, these guys made a decision and they stuck with that decision until they had completed the vision they saw in their minds.

Decision comes from Latin *decisio* and literally means "to cut off". Whenever you make a real decision you are cutting off all other options, and the only thing that remains is your choice. Stop waffling and wondering. The longer you hesitate, the more the Universe will bring you evidence of your lack of clarity. Decide what you want, decide to make it so, and that's that. Go after it every single day and it must come about if you but stick to your decision.

2.6.6. Be Who You Wish to Become

One of the most common misconceptions about the Law of Attraction is that it responds to and brings you what you desire. This really couldn't be more inaccurate.

The Law of Attraction responds to and brings you who you **BE** in every single moment of every single day.

I say "who you be" because *be* is a verb that rests in the present moment. If I say "who you *are*" instead of using the word "be", I'm implying that you are a fixed individual that cannot change, and that's not how it works. In every single moment you are broadcasting to the Universe who you be in that particular moment by the thoughts you are entertaining.

Therefore, we find that if you wish to experience financial abundance, who you BE in the majority of your moments must be someone who experiences financial abundance. You have to feel as if your desires were *already your reality*, and then begin altering your habits and character in order to become that person.

If you believe that just because you desire a Ferrari and you visualise it in your garage that it will magically appear, you are mistaken. What must occur if you really desire the Ferrari, is you must become the person that would own a Ferrari. The Law of Attraction really is much more practical and "realistic" than many of the books and movies make it out to be.

There will always be a logical, step-by-step process from where you currently are to the manifestation of your desires. It may take years for you to become the person who owns a Ferrari, but if you are persistent it **must** happen, it can't not happen.

Another very misguided assumption about the Law of Attraction is that no action is necessary on your part, that the Universe will just plop that Ferrari into your garage. Wrong! Your physical action is an absolutely necessary component of how the Law of Attraction works. It works through you, and through the world around you.

For example, 2 + 2 = 4. 4 is your Ferrari, 2 is the Universe, and the other 2 is you. If you take your 2 out of the equation, you can't possibly reach 4. Make sense? Your action and efforts are a necessary component to the law of attraction equation.

How to BE Differently

Whenever you observe something in your reality, whether it is wanted or unwanted, you immediately offer a vibration that is congruent with that situation. So if you look at an empty bank account, you will automatically radiate 'brokeness' to the Universe, and that's exactly what will be delivered to you. So if you want to create something new, you must cease giving your attention to the empty bank account or anything that reminds you of 'brokeness'.

"But wait . . ." you say, "then how do I create something new without giving attention to what I don't want? Especially when what I don't want is everywhere in my reality?"

And I say, "good question".

It's a bit of a tricky situation. You must first accept full responsibility for your situation, and that means that you can't turn your back on it and deny its existence. If you attempt to deny its existence, you would be denying that you created it which makes you powerless to create something else. On the other hand, anytime you observe it and take responsibility for it, you immediately offer the vibration of it which brings more!

The answer lies in what is called creative observation. The idea is to give your current situation momentum in the direction which you want it to go.

For example, let's say that you're currently broke and you really want to experience abundance. Every time anything shows up in your reality related to finances, you must observe it getting better and better and better. You must know that even though you're still broke, your situation is continually improving in the direction that you desire. In your mind you must *create* the evidence that your situation is improving. Without sincerely attempting to do this, your situation will remain the same. You cannot turn your back on reality, and when you do, you delude yourself. The answer lies in always knowing that your situation is improving, that's how you *BE* differently.

The Law of Attraction isn't a magic pill that instantly gives you what you want. The Universe doesn't operate by quick fixes. I want you to have realistic expectations whenever you begin consciously working with the Universe, because I am well aware of all the shallow information that is floating around. Anytime anybody tells you that they have the quick fix to your problems, immediately turn and run in the other direction. It doesn't and never will exist.

2.6.7. The Importance of Faith

Faith is one of the most important aspects of working with your mind and the Universe to create a life of your choosing.

Whenever I use the word 'faith', I am not referring to any type of religious or dogmatic faith. Faith is a much stronger word for belief, and consequently, is much stronger than mere wishing or hoping. The majority of us sometimes have trouble creating our lives because we never take the time to cultivate faith in our dreams. We sit around and *hope* that it may happen, or we *wish* that things will turn out in our favour, but these emotions are too weak to stimulate the Universe into action on our behalf.

If you do not truly believe that what you are going after (your goal or dream) is going to be attained, then it likely never will. On a very practical level, it should be quite apparent that if you don't really believe you can achieve something, then you wouldn't take constructive action towards its end. Belief, or faith, creates certainty and forward motion, while disbelief creates hesitancy and chaotic action.

Because of the belief required to create something in your life, it is often easier to begin working with the Law of Attraction by intending something easily believable. It is much easier to manifest a quarter then it is a million dollars if you've never worked with the law before. Ironically, the Universe doesn't care whether you want to create $1,000 or $1,000,000, it will give you whatever you ask for so long as you have *complete faith* that it will come about.

The fantastic thing about faith is that it isn't something static that you possess, or lack, from birth onward. Like everything in this book, **faith is a skill that can be learned and mastered.** Faith can most easily be created through the processes of auto-suggestion and persistence.

Auto-suggestion is the process of consciously choosing your self-talk. You have the choice of saying whatever you want to your mind, and if you wish to develop faith you must continually tell yourself that you have faith. This is where persistence comes into play. You cannot reasonably expect to have faith in your vision by telling yourself that you have faith only a couple of times. In order for faith to be cultivated, you must continue to talk of faith in your vision (in your own mind) over and over again until your desired end comes about.

This may sound like a lot of work, and it is depending on how you look at it. Personally, I make sure that I only choose a vision that I am so absolutely enthused about that I have no problem whatsoever taking the time to cultivate faith. I pick an idea so tantalising that I'll do whatever it takes to achieve it, and I think that's the key to developing faith. If you just kind-of sort-of want something, it's doubtful that you'll do what's necessary to develop faith.

Through enough repetition, you literally convince yourself that your vision will become real, and then you're home free from that point forward.

Being persistent and sticking to your idea requires going against the grain. This is difficult especially at first but it's absolutely necessary. This initial process of persistence is sort of like a test from the Universe. It wants to know if you're serious about your vision and so it waits. It waits to see if you'll give up in the face of difficulty and only once you have proved that you will never give up will the Universe shower upon you all that you have dreamed of.

Let go of the past, and let go of your present circumstances. Do not cling to what has been in fear of the unknown. If your dream is to become your reality, you must leave behind what you have known up to this point, and courageously embrace the mystery that lays ahead. Place your faith in the Universe, or whatever Higher Power you may believe in, and know that you will always be taken care of. This faith in yourself and your Higher Power will serve to keep you treading forward in the face of difficulty.

2.6.8. How to Hold a New Vibe

Now we get to the nitty-gritty specific strategies of working with the Law of Attraction. Understand that these strategies are only effective to the degree that you understand the previous sections in this chapter. While you can use these processes to begin changing your reality, you can use them much more effectively if you understand why exactly they work.

Your vibe is your overall signal that you are sending out into the Universe at any given moment in time. A vibe can be described as the feeling you have as a result of your frequency of vibration. Words such as happy, joyful, flowing, or dark, constricted, fearful, etc., can all be ways to describe a particular vibe or vibrational frequency. As we discussed, your vibration controls your reality by attracting what is congruent, and repelling that which is incongruent.

Your vibe fluctuates throughout the day, but you generally have one dominant vibe that you return to over and over again. Think of your dominant vibe like your home; at times you may leave your home and venture into other areas, but you always eventually return. It is your dominant vibe that controls your reality. **Dominant** is the key word here, and it means your vibe that is present over 50% of the time.

If you wish to alter your reality, you must move to a new home. You must willingly pack up your things and leave your old house. You must shift your dominant vibe from what it currently is to one that is congruent with the reality you wish to create. Just like moving to a new city, this vibe shifting is not an easy process. You will encounter feelings of nervousness, fear, uncertainty, and discomfort as you venture into previously unexplored territory.

All it takes for you to move to a new place of residence is to hold the new vibe for over fifty percent of your time spent awake on a consistent basis. Eventually, your new vibe will take hold and you will have successfully moved to a new home.

The Practice

There are many ways to go about holding a new vibe. Some of these strategies include visualisation, listening to your favourite music, watching the sunset, spending time in nature, playing with your family, etc. Anything that temporarily transports you to a better feeling place is something that is positively affecting your vibration.

It's rather easy to alter your vibration in any given moment, the more difficult part occurs whenever you realise that this new vibration must become your **dominant** one. Holding an appreciation for instance is quite easy whenever you go for a walk and it's a beautiful day outside. However, holding onto that same vibe of appreciation is much more difficult as you move through your working day. It's difficult but it's most certainly doable.

If you decide that you wish to create a new reality for yourself, you must commit to finishing up front. The Universe doesn't respond to a half effort as much as we all wished that it did. Think of it like going into space:

The current planet you're on is your current dominant vibration, and its gravitational pull keeps you on that planet. This allows you to explore other areas, but you'll always be on that planet. Your new vibe (abundance for instance) can be likened to another planet that you wish to go to. In order to leave your current planet (vibe), you must exert enough force with enough consistency that you escape the gravitational pull. If you peter out before you've rocketed past the current gravitational pull, then you won't go anywhere but back down to your planet.

This really reveals the importance of persistent effort. It's quite alright if you mess up here and there, and actually that's expected; none of us are anywhere close to perfect. But the difference between those that pull this off, and those that don't, is the awareness of when they're off track, and the willingness to do whatever it takes to get back on track.

Visualisation

Visualisation is the most effective strategy that I have personally come across to shift my dominant vibe.

The basic idea is that you are going to travel mentally to where you really want to be, while at the same time disconnecting with where you are. What this does is it brings your future aspirations into your present moment so you can get a head on how you'll be whenever your new reality is real.

You need **at least thirty minutes daily** to devote to this practice. If you aren't willing to carve out a measly thirty minutes to change your life, then I'd bet against you ever changing at all. As with anything related to personal development, the first most important thing is the decision and the willingness to grow.

Carve out thirty minutes a day, fifteen minutes right after you wake up and fifteen minutes right before you go to bed. This isn't a tremendous amount of work and you'll be astonished by the results you'll enjoy from a sincere effort.

1. Identify a place for your visualisation that is as least physically stimulating as possible (i.e. no noise, no light, room temperature, no interruptions, etc.)
2. Sit in a comfortable position with your back completely straight (you can sit on the floor or a chair, the most important thing is a straight back)
3. Set a timer (I use my phone while keeping it on silent so there are no interruptions) for fifteen minutes and then start it
4. Close your eyes and inhale through your nose all the way down to the bottom of your stomach for a count of five; then hold the breath for a count of ten and then exhale through your mouth until

there is no air leftover in your lungs. Perform five cycles of this deep breathing to calm yourself

5. Now begin to create a mental image of exactly who you wish to become and the life that you wish to live. This may require a significant amount of time as you play around with idea after idea in your mind. You don't necessarily have to "see" it, but just do whatever comes naturally to you. Visualise this new you, and your new life as if it were already happening (this means don't make it a fantasy or put it off into the future). Make it as real as possible by including minute details and attempting to feel it

6. With some practice (two-three weeks), you will identify a sort of feeling basis for this new you and your new reality. You'll find a feeling place that feels normal in the context of your visualisation and this is your new vibe

7. With some more practice, you'll be able to load up and experience your new vibe in shorter amounts of time. The more time you spend experiencing your new vibe, the quicker your reality will shift around you

8. Begin loading up this new vibe throughout your day (e.g. whenever you go to the restroom load it up, whenever you brush your teeth load it up,

whenever you get into your car load it up, etc.). You can load up your new vibe by taking your visualisation and selecting one tiny piece of it that represents how you want to be, and then taking a few seconds to run through it mentally

9. Put forth a sincere effort to spend more and more of your time in this new vibe, and over time it will take hold and it will eventually become your dominant vibe

10. After you reach the tipping point where the majority of your time is rooted in your new vibe, your life will begin to change rapidly. From this point forward all you can do is let go and have faith that everything will work out just fine

This practice is extremely valuable, and as soon as the third week you'll begin noticing that you're acting differently. Your actions are an effect of your dominant vibration, and by altering your vibration, even a little bit, you begin to alter your actions.

Become aware of any new ideas or thoughts that seem to originate from your new vibration, and act on them immediately. These are the ideas that will take you from where you are to where you want to be.

You might feel some fear or massive discomfort as your life begins to shift. This is okay and completely normal.

You'll be transitioning from a life that you have known for quite some time, into the unknown. Uncertainty is something that typically frightens us. If you allow fear to get the best of you, you will block the shift and your life won't change one bit. It's a bit of a leap of faith wherein you don't know exactly what's going to happen, but you're willing to find out. Trust in yourself, the Universe, and know that the life you have identified as what you desire is right for you. Don't allow petty fears stop you from becoming who you know you're meant to be.

2.7

CHAPTER 9:
ABUNDANCE AND PROSPERITY

2.7.1. Introduction

Abundance is one of those topics that is given a lot of attention in the field of personal development. It goes without saying that one of the most sought after aspects of a successful life is experiencing the financial abundance that goes right along with it.

There is a commonly held belief that says wanting to obtain wealth is an evil pursuit; it is this single belief alone that has caused more poverty than anything else. Right from the get go it's important to understand that money is what it is. By that, I mean that money has no inherent qualities. It is not evil, nor is it good. It simply is what it is. The qualities that money will take on are completely dependent upon how the person uses it. You can use money for good and noble causes, or you can use money for ignoble pursuits. It's all up to you. The problem arises when we hear story after story about the people that do hideously evil things to gain more wealth. We have a widespread belief that in order to earn a lot of money you have to bad things, and this holds us back.

Again, this is a case of false beliefs that we have been told to accept since our early years. Often, the lower and middle classes come up with excuses in order to justify their lack of financial security.

They say things such as:

- Money isn't everything you know
- Money can't buy you happiness
- Money isn't that important
- The rich are just greedy people
- Money is bad
- It is bad to have so much whenever so many have so little
- I'm too young to earn a lot of money
- I'm not educated enough to be wealthy
- I'm not good enough to earn tremendous amounts of money

These thoughts are nothing but excuses. Instead of summoning the courage required to fix their financial situation, they rely upon these to justify their current position. It's much easier to excuse oneself instead of taking progressive action. This is fine if you really don't want to earn a lot of money; however, if you would like to experience wealth then you must become aware that these beliefs will hold you back.

Perhaps the most destructive belief is that we are not worthy of financial abundance. This is a very deep belief that often lies at the root of all money problems. For some odd reason we feel that we aren't worthy of being rich, or living a rich life. Understand that you are worthy of every single thing you could ever want in this life. There is nothing you have to do to become worthy, you already are.

In this chapter we're going to explore the idea of abundance as it applies to all areas of life, not just finances. There is abundance in relationships, health, ideas, fun, and every other area of our lives.

Experiencing abundance begins with a particular mindset. If you are currently experiencing poverty, or if you feel a sense of lack in your life, then it's safe to say that you have not yet adopted the proper mindset. This is okay and very normal as it's the social norm to believe in and experience lack. It is only those few that have decided to create a better lives for themselves that experience true abundance. You must be willing to go against the grain and be okay being the odd one out. As with anything, results can only be obtained over a period of consistent, persistent effort. You will make mistakes and there's absolutely no shame in that. The important thing is that you get up, dust yourself off, and get back on the horse.

2.7.2. The Abundance Mindset

As we discussed briefly in the introduction, abundance itself is about much more than experiencing financial wealth. In its essence, abundance is about living in harmony with the expansiveness, and infinite nature, of your true self. When you live within the realisation of your true abundant nature, it is physically manifested in financial abundance, love abundance, fun abundance, friendship abundance, etc.

As a conscious human being, you must begin to realise that you are so much more than how you typically identify yourself. Most of us tend to think of ourselves as nothing more than our bodies, in which we exist as some sort of soul or mental entity. This is the commonly held idea of ourselves, and it's inaccurate.

Who you really are is a piece of a greater whole. We are all consciousness, and our personal identity is simply this greater consciousness focused into a particular perspective. Whenever you live with the idea that you are separate from everything around you, then the common experience is that of lack. It is only when you begin to align your way of looking at yourself with universal truth, that you can begin to experience the joy and abundance that is your birthright.

What science is currently telling us and what the mystics have always told us is that the Universe is infinite. Infinite!

Put down this book for a second and try and grasp just how large "infinite" is. Mentally picture yourself expanding beyond your body, beyond this planet that we live on, and all the way out into the cosmos. We are all constantly growing and evolving because of our infinite nature. There literally is no end to who we are. If you can realise this, and then realise that you are not separate from this infiniteness but an integral part of it, then you will begin to experience abundance.

Do you think the infinite Universe is *ever* worried about a lack of resources? Absolutely not! Do you realise that you are the infinite Universe? Then why would you ever worry about a lack of resources? The only reason why you do worry about a lack of resources is because you have been taught that worry is the only way. All throughout life you have heard people talk about lack and limitation; it's on the news, your parents talk about it, and so do your friends. It is only a very few individuals that have risen above such narrow beliefs.

The belief in scarcity perpetuates our sense of competition in the world. "Go to university and get as educated as you can so you can beat out the competition for the limited well-paying jobs!" they say. And once you get that job, "you've got to work nights and weekends if you really want to win!" This idea of competition comes from the belief that there is a financial pie. This pie is only so big and in order for you to obtain wealth, you've got to compete for a bigger piece of the pie. This sounds logical right? Well it is for the average individual, and that's why the average individual is barely scraping by.

Release the idea of competition, and replace it with the idea of creation. All you must do is focus on developing your ability to create value for the world around you, and the amount of money that you can earn is unlimited.

Understand that it is worry and belief in lack that creates the scarcity that you may be experiencing. If you will stop believing in a lack of anything, then it must disappear from your experience.

So how do I adopt an abundance mindset?

The abundance mindset is more than a particular set of thoughts. It's much more than thinking about yourself and your life in a certain manner. Your thoughts, or mindset, is actually more of an effect in the first place. The real cause of an abundance mindset is your emotional heart-set, or how you truly *feel* deep within you.

Perhaps the most telling of these emotions is the emotion of complete appreciation. Appreciation is the emotion of loving and accepting every single thing in yourself and the magnificent Universe around you. It's a feeling of complete elation at the chance to experience another day on this wondrous planet.

It is this emotion that stimulates and gives birth to the mindset that is often thought of as the cause of abundance.

Thus, we find that the most important pursuit for you at the outset is the cultivation of an abundant heart-set. After you have successfully switched your emotions from those of lack to those of abundance, you can then fine tune your experience by fine tuning your thoughts.

Below are some strategies that I have used with effectiveness to begin realising my true nature, and the reality of abundance. Choose what you are most drawn to and experiment:

- **Meditation**—The idea of meditation is to go beyond words and experience yourself as you truly are beyond your mental activity. It is the experience of complete inner silence. This practice begins to help you realise that abundance really is your birth right, and it is who you are at your most basic level. You begin to see that your belief in lack is nothing but thoughts that you have repeated your entire life. Meditation is the first step to changing yourself, because for the first time you'll realise that you are more than what you've been living as

- **Journaling**—Take time each day to write *positively* about your life. By looking for and identifying the good that surrounds you, you are placing your attention on positivity. The more you place your attention on anything, the more its presence grows in your life. Therefore, the simple act of focusing on abundance and positive ideas, for ten or fifteen minutes a day, will expand its presence in your life. There is always something positive in your life no matter how bad you think your life is. Search for things that you could appreciate if you wanted to and focus on that

- **Belief**—Take some time to think of the most successful people you admire. Realise that you are exactly the same as them, no more and no less. We are all human beings and we all have the same potential for success. The difference between these successful individuals, and those of us that don't succeed is the exercise of that potential. In order for you to begin tapping into your infinite potential, a belief in yourself is first required. With belief, you'll give your full efforts; on the flip side, without a belief in yourself you won't even give it a shot

- **Resources**—Begin the daily habit of reading and consuming ideas that stem from abundance. As you first consume these ideas, they may feel off to you because you aren't in resonance. However, by continually listening to these ideas they will start to influence your mind, and your predominant paradigm will subtly begin to shift. Try and get a bead on how these successful individuals think and feel about life. Once you identify their paradigms, do the work required to adopt them as your own

By taking these four simple strategies and applying them to your life, you can begin to move towards abundance in all areas of your life. This will take time and effort, but the rewards far outweigh the effort necessary to realise them. Give it your best for at least three months and see how far you'll go in that short period of time. Any less than three months of solid effort won't be enough to see any results, and you'll end up discouraged. Tap into the power within you to remain consistent and you'll soon experience the life that you desire.

2.7.3. Appreciation is the Key

Gratitude is one of the greatest aspects of living a successful life. It really doesn't matter what hardships you may have faced thus far, for you always possess the ability to appreciate everything in your life. Appreciation in this way floods your life with joy and opportunities. It's as if the Universe is waiting for you to see the beauty in what's currently around you before it will give you more.

Even though appreciation brings more good into your life, its most profound impact is on your being. When you live from appreciation you feel absolutely amazing; you fly high and nothing has the ability to bring you down. You see the joy in everything and everyone, and this dramatically alters your interactions with the world around you. This gratitude changes your attitude towards others and the world in a way that creates joyful experiences left and right.

From the perspective of the Law of Attraction, it makes perfect sense that appreciation would bring great experiences into your life. Whenever you radiate the emotion of gratitude you are telling the Universe that you are thankful for whatever you're experiencing. The Universe must then, by law, deliver to you more that will make you feel that exact same way.

The tricky part is first cultivating appreciation when you don't feel that you have much to appreciate. You must alter your habitual emotions before the Universe will alter what it delivers to you.

Most of us live with the belief that we can't appreciate any aspect of our lives until everything is perfect; we are always chasing the false idea of perfection. We assume that perfection is something that actually exists, and only once we reach it will our lives be good enough for us to be happy. I see this in myself just as much as I see it in almost every person around me; there is always *something else* . . .

- After I graduate university then I can be happy
- Once I find a girlfriend/boyfriend I'll really appreciate life
- After this exam is over I can finally relax and enjoy myself
- Etc.

The common thread in all of these examples is that we are pushing happiness and appreciation into the future when they can only exist in the present moment.

The effects of this kind of thinking devastates our ability to experience abundance and fundamental joy. Without appreciation, life loses its sparkle and its wonder. With appreciation, life opens up and you begin to experience the true joy of living.

There is so much to appreciate in everyday life. It only takes a willingness to feel grateful, and you'll be sure to find a reason. There truly is such magnificence all around us!

- The Earth is still spinning in orbit around the sun
- The sun came up today
- You are alive and get to experience life
- You have eyes that can read this book and observe the beauty around you
- You have challenges in your life that you get to overcome in order to become stronger
- You are breathing

It's important to understand that appreciation, just like abundance, is your natural state of being. We are taught from early in life to think in ways that restrict our natural appreciation for life, and that is why so many of us seem to dread each day. Understand that it is only your thoughts that are holding the good that you deserve away from you.

The most destructive of these learned thought patterns is that of focusing on *not enough* and what's *wrong*. A focus on these subjects will always bring more of it into your life, and thus, it should be avoided at all costs. It is not until your thoughts of *not enough* are released from your mind that *enough* can be your experience.

2.7.4. How to Cultivate Appreciation

Appreciation is a habit of mind that can be practiced and learned just like any other skill. The development of this skill requires sufficient awareness to be able to notice and control your emotions. Though it may take time to learn how to willingly stimulate a feeling of thankfulness, it is a practice that will serve you for the rest of your life.

In this section I want to discuss specific strategies and tactics that you can use in order to cultivate the habit of appreciation. In order for gratitude to become your habitual way of interacting with the world, it's critical that you make it just that, a habit. Start small with just one of the strategies you'll find in this chapter, and do it every single day for thirty days until it becomes automatic. I

CARLA SCHESSER

would rather you start small with just five minutes a day than try to adopt three different strategies and quickly fall off the wagon. Don't bite off more than you can chew. You know your capabilities and how much is too much. Start small and work your way up.

The Strategies

Gratitude Journal—A gratitude journal is a very simple strategy used to introducing appreciation into the mind. The practice is this; take just ten minutes a day and write down everything you can think of that you appreciate. It can be on any subject, event, person, etc. The whole idea is to look hard and find things that you appreciate. This practice is incredibly valuable because as you begin to spend more of your time searching for things to appreciate, more of the things that you do appreciate will appear in your life. Buy a journal and start with listing things you appreciate for just ten minutes a day; try and list twenty to thirty different things. Execute this practice at the same time every day in order to establish it as a habit (I find the early morning to work very well for me).

Meditation—Meditation is by far the most beneficial habit that I have ever installed into my daily routine. I highly, highly, highly recommend that you experiment

174

with meditation. Many people view meditation as some weird religious ritual with robes and strange chanting; nothing could be farther from the truth. Meditation is simply the act of quieting the mind. It is deceptively difficult, but the benefits have to be experienced to be understood. When you meditate you slow down your mind and begin to connect with yourself and everything around you. You get back to your fundamental being. As you spend more and more time just being, appreciation begins to flood into your mind and your body. You will literally be able to feel the appreciation in your being, it's a really neat experience. Start with just ten minutes a day at the same time every day and progress from that point.

Presence—No problems exist in the present moment. If you are fully in the present moment there are no thoughts in your mind, and thus, no problems to be aware of. All of our problems are nothing but creations of our mind, and as we relax into the present moment these fictitious problems evaporate. Your presence will increase naturally as a result of your meditation practice. In its essence, the practice of presence is the practice of meditation extended into daily life. It is the quieting of the mind as you perform your daily duties, and an opening up to the brilliance of everything that is life. For the first time since you were a child, you will actually experience reality without any mental obstructions thus returning your awe of this life experience.

Perceptions—Your perceptions of your life actually create your life, and determine your emotional states. Therefore, we can see that if you don't commonly experience appreciation for your life, then you are viewing your world in a way that isn't congruent with thankfulness. Fortunately, all that's required to experience gratitude is a change in your perceptions. When you begin to look at life with an empowering perspective, you release your victim mentality and begin to step into your natural power.

- Begin to view your life as the wonderful gift it is and appreciate your *aliveness* each and every day
- Begin to look upon your problems not as something unwanted, but as opportunities to grow
- Actively search out and identify the positive in every single negative situation (there is always good no matter how badly you don't want to see it)

When you begin to see the good in every seemingly "bad" situation, you gain the ability to appreciate your life regardless of what's happening. This is one of the most valuable skills you could ever develop.

A change in your perceptions allows you to realise that your emotions aren't dependent on the circumstances that surround you. Instead of giving your power away to what's happening around you, you step up and take control of your being. Develop the perspective of being grateful for the opportunity to live, and your life will take on a completely new flavour.

Associations—This strategy goes back to a previous chapter in the book when we discussed the affect that your associations have on your life. To reiterate, you take on the attitudes and perspectives of those people that you spend most of your time with. If you wish to cultivate appreciation as a habit in your life, begin to associate with those people that already experience consistent gratefulness.

As difficult as it is, release your connections with those people that do not appreciate their own lives. You aren't necessarily severing the friendship for good, but you are severing the friendship until that person develops the kind of attitude that you yourself want. There are many meet-ups and groups of individuals all around the world that live in a constant state of appreciation. Begin to insert yourself into such groups, and you will begin to take on their attitudes as your own.

Positive Messages—You take on the flavour of the dominant inputs in your life. By consciously exposing yourself to positive messages you will become positive yourself and appreciation will slowly become your natural way of being. Find the most joyful people, and listen to what they have to say. Allow not only their words, but their radiance, penetrate your consciousness to the point where you begin to emulate that way of being. As humans we tend to emulate one another, so it's vital that you consciously choose who you will emulate and who you will not. The choice is yours. Take fifteen to twenty minutes a day and listen to a quality personal development program. You can do this while you're exercising, grocery shopping, etc. so you don't have to spend any extra time installing this habit.

Daily Routines—One of the most effective strategies I have come across is practicing appreciation right after I wake up, and right before I go to bed. I have made it a habit to wake up and immediately begin expressing my appreciation for anything I can find to appreciate. This develops momentum in the direction I want it to go, and is the meaning of ""starting the day off on the right foot," or "waking up on the right side of the bed".

Post a reminder by your bed, on your ceiling, or on your phone, and begin the practice of appreciation before you start your day. This practice alone can completely turn your life around. Take a short five minutes before you even get out of bed and before you go to sleep to focus on things you appreciate. Let your problems be, and just focus on what you're grateful for. Give it a sincere effort for thirty days and your life will never be the same.

*   *   *

These are just a few strategies that you can begin using right this day to cultivate more appreciation in your life. Take the time, and put forth the effort necessary to alter your habitual way of viewing the world. Appreciation is an absolutely wonderful emotion to experience, and its effects on your life will astound you. Take the leap of faith and just give it a try. Experiment and see what comes of it; I think you'll be pleasantly surprised.

2.7.5. How to Experience Financial Abundance

Almost every single person in our society today wants to have the experience of financial abundance. Money is not necessary for a happy life. However, in our lives today money means freedom, and freedom is one of the most fundamental pursuits of the human species. By finding the feelings of freedom in your life that already exist, you can begin calling abundance into your life.

Find this sense of freedom by realising that:

- You have the ability to choose your work
- You have complete control over how you spend your time
- You can choose which thoughts you will think
- You choose your friends

Look at all this freedom! Even if you haven't been exercising your freedom in these and other areas of your life, that doesn't take it away from you. As you begin to exercise your freedom in these seemingly small parts of your life, you increase the role of freedom in your experience.

Perhaps the most common mistake that holds so many of us to poverty is the belief that financial abundance is an event. How many times have you dreamed about winning the lottery or coming into a great inheritance from some unknown aunt or uncle? These kinds of fantasies quickly point out the mindset that is holding you away from the abundance you desire.

Financial abundance is a ***process***. It is not an ***event***.

If you see those that are fabulously wealthy and ascribe their fortune to luck, then you believe wealth is an event. You think that wealth is something that just happens to the "lucky" few, and the only way for you to achieve wealth is by a sudden turn of fate.

In reality, achieving financial abundance is a long process. It can be compared to achieving a fit body; you know that the reason someone has an amazing body is because they have put the time and effort into building it. You wouldn't ascribe someone's levels of fitness to luck, that would be ridiculous! It's the exact same with wealth. Someone's level of wealth isn't a result of luck, rather it's a result of time and effort that that person has put in.

You're not alone if you look in yourself and find that you do actually think abundance is an event. We are raised to think this way and that's why the majority of us aren't where we want to be financially. Money follows certain rules and laws that if you come into alignment with, will increase your wealth position tremendously. Release the idea that wealth is only achieved by luck, and it happens all at once. Building wealth is a process of persistence that may take years of time and effort, never forget this.

Beliefs and Money

Your beliefs about money will be the determining factor in how much money you'll have flowing through your life. Unfortunately, money is the single most misunderstood subject that we encounter on a daily basis. We have so many conflicting thoughts and beliefs that it's no wonder we never achieve true wealth. These beliefs are mainly adopted from those around us in our early years. Realise now that if you were raised by people who were not wealthy, you likely will not be wealthy unless you work internally on your thoughts and beliefs.

I want to provide you a list of some of the most common negative beliefs regarding money. If you recognise any of these as familiar, then it's a good chance that you have adopted them as your own. If you even partially agree with any of these statements, then your amount of financial abundance will be forever limited until you release these ideas. These are the most insidious ideas you could hold about money, and they must be eliminated if wealth is to be experienced.

- Money is bad
- The rich are greedy and dishonest
- Money is the root of all evil
- Money can't buy happiness
- Money doesn't grow on trees
- We can't afford that
- You have to be very smart to be rich
- Being poor is more noble and spiritual than being rich
- There is only so much money in the world
- A penny saved is a penny earned

- You have to work really hard to be rich
- Money is not spiritual
- You need lots of money to make lots of money

That's a pretty solid list of common beliefs about money and none of them are supportive or even logical! It's not "bad" if you believe in some of these ideas, and it is completely your choice if you wish to continue believing them. The point I am trying to make is that every single one of these ideas will seriously limit the amount of money that will be present in your life.

If you want to experience financial abundance, begin at once to uncover your thoughts about money. Make a list of your money beliefs and go through them one by one to identify if they will either help or hinder you on your wealth journey. This is an extremely important part of increasing your financial position, and you can experience tremendous gains after eliminating only one of these unhelpful ideas.

Money is Energy

There is not a limited supply of money in the Universe. If you think that there is a limited amount of money, then you will by necessity think that you have to compete for your share. You'll have to beat out others to secure your share of the pie. This puts you at odds with your fellow human beings, and ultimately ensures financial struggle.

Money is energy just like everything else in the Universe, and energy is of infinite supply. Money is the physical manifestation of the amount of energy you are allowing into your life. This is why whenever you are experiencing financial difficulty, you will feel very tight and restricted in your inner being. This is because you're restricting the flow of energy into your life.

Open yourself up and allow energy to flow through you. You are a conductor of Universal energy and money is only one form of this energy.

Money can be compared to water. Allow money to flow into and out of your life like a stream, but always increasing in intensity and amount. How silly would you look if you went to the closest river and tried to grab handfuls of water and hold onto them? Incredibly silly, yet this is exactly what people do when it comes to money. They don't allow money to flow, and they fight and struggle to hold onto the equivalent of water. It is this fight and struggle that is felt as restriction within the body.

Instead of grasping at water with your hands, it might be smarter to instead build channels and canals to direct the water where you want it to go. The harder you try to grab money the more it eludes you. By increasing your understanding of how money works, you can spend your time building irrigation canals instead of unsuccessfully trying to grasp at money.

"How do you build these canals?" you ask. The key word here is *value*. By utilising your specific strengths, your time, and your efforts to provide value to society, you are in effect building your irrigation canals. You must build your canals before the water will flow, and this is why we see that wealth is a process and not an event. You cannot snap your fingers and immediately have a completed canal. The building of the canal is the process that eventually provides you the abundance of water that you seek.

In order to build your canal deeper and longer, improve the tools that you are using. You can only work so hard, and hard work alone won't build a large canal. If you are only using your hands, you can build and dig until your days are done while not building much of anything special. However, if you take the time to develop and use effective tools, you can multiply your work and thereby get more returns from the same amount of effort. The wealthy know that wealth is about working intelligently, and rarely about working hard.

All of this should give you a very broad understanding of how money works. This section is meant to give you a bird's eye view of the subject of money. This overarching view is essential before we get into the specific money strategies which we will cover in the next section.

2.7.6. Financial Strategies

Now that we've taken a good look at the subject of money from a higher perspective, it's time to get into the details of how to increase your wealth position. There are a few specific strategies that you'll find almost every extremely wealthy person follows.

There are only two ways to earn money and they are:

1. Work for money
2. Have your money work for you

The wealthy understand this, and they put their money to work for them. The poor don't understand this, and they spend their entire lives working for their money which is the most inefficient way to become wealthy. Of course as you are starting out in life, it is necessary that you work for money. However, the sooner you start putting your money to work for you, the sooner you gain the freedom to decide if you want to work at all!

Each and every single dollar can be thought of as a freedom fighter in your freedom army. If you habitually spend your money without saving any, you are throwing your precious freedom fighters away and you'll have a much smaller army with which to achieve freedom. The most intelligent use of money is putting it to work so that you earn without direct action.

The wealthy also understand that trading time for dollars is the worst strategy there is to earning money. This strategy is the most common one within our society, and that's why there is such an obsession with jobs. I'll admit it, after I had my first job there was no way I could ever have one again. I resisted the idea of giving someone control over my time and efforts, and that hasn't changed since then. The wealthy know that they can only achieve great wealth by separating their time from their income; this allows them to earn money while they're sleeping, while they're eating, while they're on vacation, and while they are doing anything.

You have most likely been told your entire life that you have to get a job, and that's the way the world works. But I want you to know that that's not true. You are more than capable of earning money doing work that you choose and want to do, without having someone over you telling you what to do. The most common vehicle to wealth for the extremely wealthy is a business which then feeds funds into carefully chosen investments. The wealthy take the time to build business systems that operate independent from their efforts. Imagine what you could do in life if you didn't have to spend your time earning money. Imagine gaining back eight hours a day to spend however you want to! The implications of these wealthy ideas are staggering to the mind and run so contrary to the commonly accepted social paradigm.

Keep these ideas in mind as you move through your life. Obviously it is not within the scope of this book for me to explain to you how to set up, build, and run an income generating system. However, if you have this idea in mind and look for opportunities, you will surely find them.

The wealthy also understand that having only one source of income is a terrible strategy. It's funny, we're taught growing up that security is the most important thing we could ever achieve in this life. Then we're told that a job is the most secure way to earn money. Let's think about that for a second though . . .

- How secure are you if your income is completely out of your control?
- How secure are you if someone can turn off your income in an instant through no fault of your own?
- How secure are you if you're a slave to a company's demands regardless of if you agree with them or not?

The notion of job security is an illusion that has imprisoned millions of people to dull, grey cubicles for the prime years of their lives. Why would you do work you hate for forty five years of your life so you can finally retire when you're old and worn out? Does that make any sense to you? Why not set your life up so you have the time and money to live *now* instead of putting your life off until you're too old to do anything fun. Again we encounter the idea that what is done by the majority is often a terrible strategy for successful living. Always think for yourself and question the validity of commonly accepted ideas. You'll usually find that what people do really doesn't make much sense at all.

The Money Strategies

The first essential step to increasing your financial position is taking an accurate look at where you currently stand. If you don't know where you are, then you can never know how to get to where you wish to be. It may not be comfortable to take a truthful look at your situation, especially if you've allowed your finances to run on its own up until this point. Pull up your bank account and other money management tools, and go through the following questions to get an accurate picture of where you currently stand.

- Exactly how much money do you currently have?
- Exactly how much money do you currently owe? (account for all of your debts including school, car, loans, etc.)
- What is your total monthly income?
- What is your total monthly expenditure?
- What is your current net worth? (calculated by subtracting your debts from your current monies)

Taking the time to answer these questions accurately will be a big step forward on your wealth journey. Even if you don't like the answers you see, at least you know the truth and you can stop denying your situation. It's always better to face the truth than turn your back on reality; even if it hurts. Understand that this is just your current wealth position, and that you do have the power to change it dramatically. You aren't doomed to a particular level of income or wealth for your entire life. As a thinking, creating human being, you do possess the ability to create great wealth for yourself.

The first few strategies deal specifically with the management of money that is already flowing into your life. Why would the Universe flow more money into your life if you can't properly care for the money that you are already receiving?

The basic premise of proper money management is spending less than you earn. Many people make the mistake of assuming that if they earned more, all of their financial problems would disappear. If you are in the habit of spending more than you earn, then it doesn't matter how much you earn as you'll always find a way to spend it. You will naturally increase your spending as you increase your earning unless you develop the necessary habits to prevent it. Understand that you can never achieve wealth if you are always spending what you're earning. You could be earning a million dollars per year, but if you spend a million dollars a year then your net worth is still at zero. Becoming wealthy is the process of earning, keeping, and then putting money to good use (spending money on liabilities is not a good use!).

This is where we get the idea of pay yourself first, a very common piece of advice found in the majority of wealth material. The idea is that before you spend any money on *anything*, you first set aside a percentage that is yours to keep. The percentage doesn't necessarily matter as it's the habit that makes the difference in the long run. Here's how you can make this a reality in your life:

1. Start by looking at your current income vs. expenditures and see if you are positive or negative at the end of each month

2. Cut down on unnecessary expenses until you are in the positive, even if it's just a few dollars (there will very often be expenditures that we really don't even need or use that just waste money every single month)

3. Start by saving just five percent of your income every single month. Put it into a high interest savings account, or other similar account so that you don't have easy access to it

4. As you establish the habit of saving a percentage of your income, begin to increase the amount you save. The more you save the faster you can experience true freedom in your life. Work your way up to ten percent and even farther if possible

The money you put into this savings account will begin to add up and create some serious momentum towards greater wealth. I can't even describe to you how good it feels to see your financial situation getting better and better; let's just say it's fun!

The next most important thing to keep in mind is that you only take money advice from those whose financial position you admire. Opinions are one of the cheapest commodities around, and every single person has them. They usually aren't right and will tend to lead you down paths you don't want to go. If you take money advice from someone who isn't doing so hot financially, why would you think that their advice would move you forwards on your wealth journey? I find it fascinating that we take advice from people who have no basis to give it! We get health advice from overweight and out of shape doctors, financial advice from our broke next door neighbour, and love advice from the friend that's never had a serious relationship. Before you ask anyone for advice about anything, make sure that they have the results that you admire and wish to attain.

Saving

Saving is one of the next important areas that must be mastered before you can make serious headway on your financial path. As much as the advice is thrown your way, **saving money is not the way to become wealthy!** Of course, saving money is absolutely essential to becoming wealthier. You can never increase your net worth if you're spending everything you're earning. However, cutting back on your expenses is not enough to get you where you want to go.

The best strategy for saving is cutting out the expenses that you don't really care about so you have money to invest. Saving isn't about decreasing the quality of your life! Begin looking at your expenses and see what you can cut out that you don't really care about.

- Can you cut out your cable bill?
- Can you cut out the coffee every day? Or at least some days?
- Can you wear the clothes you already have for a while?
- Can you buy e-books instead of physical books?

These are just a few examples of where you could cut back if you wanted to. Before we move on however, I want to make sure that you understand how important it is to not focus just on saving. If you applied every single one of the above examples to your life, you might only save around $2,000 a year. While that may seem like a lot of money, it really isn't. Sure it will help you invest more, but if you really want to become wealthy, you must optimise your saving strategy and then focus your efforts on **earning more**. The majority of people are always cutting back instead of spending the same amount of energy figuring out how to earn more! If you focus on earning more, you'll be able to continually improve the quality of your life while investing a large amount of money. Sounds like a much better strategy to me!

The biggest rule of the wealthy is to not spend what you don't have. If you can't afford it in cash, don't buy it. It's as simple as that. Credit card debt is the fastest way to ruin your financial life. It's a way for the big companies to take advantage of our love for instant gratification. They give us these pieces of plastic and say, "oh don't worry if you can't afford it now, just buy it and then you can pay us every month for five years until you've paid it in full!" What happens is you end up paying much more than you would have if you just paid with cash, and it drains your bank account every single month.

Credit card debt traps you and ensures that you can never stop trading your time for money. What if instead of buying things, you lived in a small apartment and only spent money on the necessities. You could potentially live on $1,100-$1,500 a month. You could earn that very easily at a part time job, thus freeing up a significant amount of your time to work on more profitable endeavours.

Finances are pretty simple with the development of self-discipline. Always keep track of where your money is going, how much you're earning, and then figure out how to lower the former and increase the latter. If you continuously do this, you'll be in a very good financial position in no time at all.

SECTION 3
THE END

3.1

CONGRATULATIONS

Well, it's about that time to say goodbye, but before I end the book I want to give you a huge congratulations. You've taken the first of many steps in what will likely be the most fulfilling journey of your life. The majority of people wouldn't have made it through this book as the majority of people are dabblers; they get caught up in an idea for a day or two at max, and then quickly let it fade. If you've gotten to this point then it's likely that you are ready to take the next steps on your ongoing journey of growth.

Seriously, it can't be understated how huge a step this is for you! Even if you didn't find anything just jaw-dropping in this book, you now have a solid idea of what areas you can now pursue to enhance your growth. Take the ideas that you found valuable and apply them to your life. Ideas are absolutely worthless without consistent application. Ignore the ideas that you didn't find valuable, but only after you've given them serious thought and consideration. As you grow, you'll find that you will consistently be attracted to the ideas that will most serve your growth at that particular time. You'll find that as you read a book through a second time, you'll take in ideas that you didn't even see before, and this is all a result of the ongoing change occurring within you.

Understand that there is no one correct path for personal development. Many of the top gurus and teachers will tell you that there is one right way, but the truth is that there are millions of different paths. The path that you will follow is the one that is right for you. You are a unique individual with different needs and wants, and as such your particular path through life will be just as unique. Take the time to get to know yourself and as you become more comfortable with who you are as an individual, you'll start to see your own path more and more clearly.

In the beginning, it is likely that instead of following your own path you have been following somebody else's path and this is completely okay. It's said that we cannot lead until we have first learned how to follow. It seems that we learn best through imitation, so imitating those that you admire can be a fast track towards your own personal growth. Read books, listen to tapes, go to seminars, and find the leaders in the field of personal development that you would really like to be like. Once you find these cats that you admire, start to pick them apart and identify their particular characteristics. As you begin to see what makes them them, begin developing yourself in those ways. This is called modelling and is a phenomenal way to improve yourself rapidly.

Take everything with grain of salt. It doesn't matter if you get an idea from your parents, your relatives, or your favourite guru; always take the idea and analyse it for yourself. Blindly accepting that which is given you will often lead you down a fuzzy path. Define your own values and decide which ideas you will accept. This will serve as your internal compass with which you will forever be able to chart your own particular course. Find what's important to you and stay true to that no matter what everyone else around you is doing. It will certainly be difficult to go against the crowd but I promise you it gets easier with time. Release your fears of being ostracised and follow your heart, it's the most important decision you'll ever make.

Most of all, learn to enjoy the journey of life. You will never reach a point where you can finally sit down and proclaim that you have reached ultimate perfection. It is our pursuit of perfection that often drives us, but don't allow this false notion to get you down when you realise that you have yet another area of your life to grow in. The joy of life is the journey of growth. Learn to live in the present moment and actually enjoy the process of growth no matter how difficult it may be. If you're always living for some future moment, you'll never be fully present; and the greatest satisfaction of life is in the present moment.

Be happy now, don't wait for this and that. Your happiness is a choice, and you have the ability to choose to be happy regardless of what's going on around you. Be happy that you're alive and you're able to experience another wonderful day on beautiful planet Earth. Take time to yourself everyday, and cultivate a lasting happiness and joy that isn't dependent on physical reality. Release your attachments to things, money, and accolades, but use them to accelerate your growth. Understand that there is nothing wrong with things or money, and that they are just as spiritual as meditation or prayer.

Take action, risk it all, and understand that in the end as you're lying on your death bed, you won't regret the mistakes you made but you'll regret the opportunities that you missed. Life is a grand adventure that is supposed to be fun and joyful. It isn't a monotonous club that will beat you down into submission. It will test you, it will challenge you, and it will see how strong you are just so you yourself can become aware of your own strength. Learn to appreciate the little things in life while dreaming of the huge things. Keep a vision before you of who you wish to become, and all in all, steadily move towards that vision one small step at a time.

Before you move on to your next growth adventure make sure that you've gotten all of the value out of this one! I've created a resources page on my website where you can find many extra goodies that weren't included in this book. You can find that here: http://carlaschesser. com.au/resources/

3.2

THANK YOU!

I want to thank you for taking the time to read this book. It really means a lot to me. There are a million and one things that you could spend your time doing, but you decided that this book was worth your attention for however long it took you to read it. There is something beautiful about the process of creation and sharing. I sincerely appreciate the opportunity I've had to create this book, and share what I've learned with you.

If there's absolutely anyway that I can help you on your path of growth, please do not hesitate to get in touch with me. My purpose with this book was to help you as much as I possibly could, and if there are still questions you may have then I would love to answer them. No question is a dumb question, and the biggest mistake is to never ask any questions.

I hope to see you around my blog and website sometime soon (http://carlaschesser.com.au). But most of all, I sincerely hope that I can continue to assist you on your own personal journey of growth for a long, long time to come.